John Norman Collins & The Michigan Murders

Barbara Hutton

Published by Trellis Publishing, 2021.

JOHN NORMAN COLLINS & THE MICHIGAN MURDERS

First edition. July 14, 2021.

Copyright © 2021 Barbara Hutton.

ISBN: 979-8224828852

Written by Barbara Hutton.

JOHN NORMAN COLLINS & THE MICHIGAN MURDERS

BARBARA HUTTON

<u>SICKO JOSEPH DUNCAN</u>

John Norman Collins/Chapman AKA "The Ypsilanti Ripper".

John Norman Collins was born on the 17th of June 1947, in Windsor, Canada but he was not set out for a happy childhood from the very beginning. Shortly after his birth, John's parents divorced and his mother Loretta and two elder siblings, brother Jerry and sister Gail, they moved across the river to Centre Line Michigan.

Much speculation surrounds the reasons for the divorce and at the very forefront, neighbours believed that Loretta had eventually plucked up the courage to leave an abusive and alcoholic husband. With her children in tow, Loretta set off for not only a new life, but quite quickly a new relationship and, shortly after her divorce from her husband, Richard, she had met and married her new love, William Collins. William would officially adopt all three children within a few years, ensuring each of them took his surname.

This new happy family life would be again, be very much short lived.

As a moth to a flame, Loretta had seemed to be always drawn to men that offered only abuse as a cornerstone to the relationship and an almost daily inebriated attitude as comfort.

But this time William also offered something extra to the wedded bliss. William was also prone and extensively keen to inflict his violent rage on his newly adopted children

Despite the gravity of the situation and their subsequent divorce when John was just 4 years old, Loretta always believed in putting her children first and in the face of difficult emotional times, she would ensure that her children's education was not tarnished. Through working tables at a local restaurant, Loretta was able to put all three children through their schooling.

But with such sacrifice and working double shifts whenever she could, it was only a matter of time before John would find only his elder brother as a typical male role model in his life..

John was enrolled at St Clements High School in Centre Line – a strict but well sought-after school. He quickly achieved academic success and became an all-round athlete. John was also captain of the football team and president of the Social C-Club. He was also a gifted pitcher for the baseball team and on the face of it, it would indeed seem that John really had everything going for him. He was well liked, polite and respected his elders.

John was also very good looking, with his chiselled features and piercing blue eyes, he would be hard to miss with his Adonis like athletic physique and his six-foot stature.

With such a resume of attributes, John was indeed, not lacking for female attention. One of his high school girlfriends, Burnadetta Hudak remarked how polite he was and that he possessed "manners galore", - holding doors open for others and standing when others entered the room; true qualities of a gentleman.

Burnadetta also suggested that Collins possessed an almost Jekyll and Hyde personality. His mood swings could become extreme, not just moody. She also commented that he was "mad most of the time". Other girlfriends also mentioned his aggressive nature, especially in his sexual mannerisms toward them.

Collins was to study next at the Eastern Michigan University in Ypsilanti. Now an honour student, John now focussed his attention on becoming a teacher.

In a nutshell, his life seemed to be well mapped out for him.

At university, John continued with his love of sports and was soon involved in many sporting activities, eventually becoming the president of the ski club. Renowned for his good looks, John was eventually approached to do some modelling work for a body building magazine, which he took on in order to earn extra money.

John's other and perhaps greatest love, was riding motorcycles, eventually owning four including his pride and joy, a Triumph. During his time at EMU, he also worked as a clerk on the University campus and joined as a member of the "Theta Chi" Fraternity Brothers.

This was to be a noticeable turning point in his young life.

The Fraternity was well known for its strict code of silence and famed for its wild parties. This was the place for co-eds to be seen.

This formalized brotherhood was also very much, a closed shop to outsiders and all members were subjected to a lifetime oath of allegiance in order to retain the ultimate in loyalty to each other.

"Theta Chi" is an international college fraternity founded in April 1856 by Arthur Chase, at Norwich, Vermont USA. It has, over the years, initiated more than 191,000 members and boasts a rattlesnake as their official motto. Although little remains public on such secretive forms of fraternities and the lengths to which members will go to protect each other, it was clearly the perfect place for John Collins to build his killing demeanour.

However, despite all the popularity, John's grades had begun to slip by the time he was 19, having put much of his attention on the fun side of university living. His once well-balanced work ethics were getting out of control. He was no longer grounded and protected by his family.

Despite his Professor telling him that he had fallen short of the necessary credits needed to achieve his Degree, John decided to skip the prescribed Summer classes in order to catch up. According to John's Professor of the time, 'John had seemed in no hurry to graduate'.

Along with his deteriorating grades, John had also been accused by other fraternity members of stealing forty dollars along with other items of value that had gone missing from the frat house. The last straw for the tight-knit fraternity came when Collins stole a motorcycle from a fellow brother and John, along with two other members was unceremoniously expelled from the main house.

John was unperturbed however and set up new accommodations with the other ex-communicated members just a block away, 619 Emmet Street.

His spiralling attitude to life seemed to have no end and soon John had begun to build up a decent sized petty criminal record with local law enforcement.

In 1967 the EMU university was to hit the headlines for all the wrong reasons.

Young Girls had started to go missing in the Ann Arbour and the Ypsilanti districts. Sexually molested corpses were found in the most debauched states; a cocktail of savage bestiality, brutal touché and frenzied blood lust were all on macabre display.

Students at the university were well known for their organized protests for black civil rights and anti-war rallies, but this time students were not only terrified, but had no real answer on how to deal with this unknown monster that had been unleashed on their once tranquil doorstep.

The First victim was Mary Fleszar who was just 19 years old. She was an EMU student and was last seen alive on July the 9th 1967. A neighbour of hers in Ypsilanti had spotted a young man in a blue/grey Chevrolet trying to offer her a lift - this was to be the last ever sighting of Mary alive. She was found by two young boys on the 7th of August 1967 on an abandoned farm in Superior Township; her body badly decomposed.

Pathologists were only able to confirm the body's identity through dental records. Marys corpse although rotting had been savagely stabbed in the breast and stomach area. She had also been savagely beaten, tortured and raped. The murderer had also hacked off her hands and feet just above the ankle. Fingers had also been sliced off with force and were never found.

Just two days after her body was found a young man turned up at the funeral home requesting to photograph her body. Staff were appalled at the distasteful request, sending the young man away in his blue/grey Chevrolet.

Victim two was Joan Elspeth Schell aged 20, an art student also from EMU.

Joan had recently moved from Plymouth to attend University and was last seen by her roommate, Susan Kolbe who had witnessed Joan hitchhiking to her boyfriend in nearby Ann Arbour and getting into a car. Her body was found by workman on the Ann Arbour roadside on the 5th of July 1968, near to where Mary had been murdered.

Her injuries were gruesome and cruel.

Joan had been repeatedly stabbed in her breasts and chest over 20 times – the depths of the stab wounds measuring four inches. Her throat was slashed, and she had a fractured skull, a result of being brutally beaten. The attacker hadn't killed her at this site, she had been dumped after death.

Other witnesses would come forward and tell of how they had seen Joan and her then neighbour, John Collins talking on the night of her disappearance. Witnesses pointed out that John only lived across the road from her at the time. Collins was questioned by police but flatly denied even knowing her, his alibi was that he had spent the weekend at his mothers' home in Centre Line and only returned on the following Monday - his alibi was never investigated nor followed up.

Victim number three was Jane Louise Mixer aged 23. Jane was a law student at EMU who had recently attached a note to the university help board asking anyone for a lift to her home in Muskegon.

Jane had been planning to tell her parents that she was getting engaged to be married, but she had failed to turn up to their home even though she left on March 20th as planned. Her naked corpse was found on March 21st, 1969 in Ann arbour where she had been dumped in a cemetery.

This time, the victim had been shot in the head and her panties and sanitary towel had been removed. Investigating officer, Detective Donald Bennett stated that "when we arrived it was a cold morning and around her neck, we could see a nylon hose, so she'd been strangled also".

During the autopsy, blood was scraped from Janes left hand and held as evidence. Witnesses state on the night of the murder, a green station wagon was seen speeding away from the cemetery. Police were unable to ever track this vehicle down.

Victim four, Maralynn Shelton, was aged just 16 years old and a high school student. She was found just a few days after Jane Mixer on the 25th of March 1969. Her naked discarded corpse was found by construction workers near the same spot where Joan Schell's remains had been dumped.

Maralynn had last been seen hitchhiking just outside of a restaurant in Ann Arbour and now, her bludgeoned lifeless body showed the devastation of her brutal beating that had taken place in what officers observed as a savage and frenzied attack. Her skull had been beaten so severely that on autopsy, it revealed that she had sustained several fractures to her skull.

This was by far the worst attack so far in the once quiet district. To stop her screams the murderer had inserted part of her skirt deep inside her throat and a garter belt had been tied tightly around her slim throat. She again had been heavily flogged as the assailant's anger grew, hacking away at her small body with a knife. The wounds were catastrophic.

To finish this unthinkable attack the murderer had also callously shoved a thick branch taken from a nearby tree and forced it into her vagina.

Victim five shockingly would put the fear of God into the community.

All the victims so far, had been subjected to the same M.O. All the victims had been young, pretty and slim with brunette coloured hair. All the corpses had been found in a 15-mile radius of Washtenaw County. All the women had an item of clothing tied around their necks. All had been stabbed around the neck area. Police felt sure that they were looking for the same monster. Perhaps more demonic and sinister was the fact that each victim had been menstruating at the time of their deaths. All except for Jane Mixer who had severe blunt force trauma but had not received stab wounds to her neck.

Dawn disappeared on the night of April 15th at 7.30pm, after visiting a friend and during what was only a short walk home. Her violated body was found the next day.

She had been savagely stabbed in her neck and chest and across her breasts. Her vagina had also received mutable stab wounds which reached round to her backside. The blouse and bra that she wore had been pushed up around her neck and her handkerchief shoved down her throat to snuff the sounds of her screams. To complete the execution and humiliation she had been strangled with an electrical cable.

Dawn was found in an abandoned farmhouse along with the jumper that she was last seen wearing. A week or so later the detectives revisited the scene only to discover that more items of her clothing had been dumped at the scene of the crime.

It was almost like the murderer was playing a game with authorities, goading them.

The crime scene and building was then set on fire and burnt to the ground, an attack of arson. whilst in the driveway leading up to the house the perpetrator had left a haunting message, a present if you like. Five carefully clipped beautiful lilac blossoms perfectly displayed for all to see. This sadistic killer was indeed enjoying his work, laughingly leaving the flowers a sick tribute to the 5 diabolical slayings he had committed.

Victim six, Alice Elizabeth Kalom was aged 23 and also a recent graduate of EMU. Her body was found in Ypsilanti on the 9th of June 1969.

Alice had been repeatedly stabbed and systematically raped. Her throat had been slashed to the extent that her spine was severed. Two gunshot wounds were found - one in her hand, a defensive wound and the other, to end her misery, a bullet had been shot into her brain.

Alice's clothes were dumped around her, but one of her shoes was missing; a potential a souvenir for the killer.

Karen sue Beineman was to be the 7th victim of this fiend.

Karen was an EMU student too and was aged just 18 years old. Her disappearance occurred on the 23rd of July. Her roommate had reported her missing to the police after she failed to return home the day after shopping for a new wig in Ypsilanti. Her body was found completely nude in a wooded gully with her breasts and stomach scalded with a type of caustic liquid.

And, just as before, her own panties had been stuffed inside her vagina. Not only were the panties covered with semen, but more ironically, contained light brown hair clippings that didn't belong to the deceased. She had also been lacerated with a knife and cut so deeply that chunks hung off her lifeless body. Alice too had been viciously beaten and repeatedly raped and strangled to death to end her torture.

Things were different this time however with the murderer leaving behind some significant clues - on purpose.

John was again playing with the police, taunting the authorities who were on the hunt for him. But his arrogance would prove his undoing and lead to his eventual apprehension. He would be free to wander no more.

A few days after the discovery of Karen's slain body, a state police corporal named "David Leik" had returned to his home after a family holiday. He found that some items in the house had been moved or were missing and decided to investigate further. Whilst putting away luggage from the trip Corporal Leik discovered the floor in his basement was covered with black paint. At first, he had though his wife's nephew had been responsible as they had asked him to stay at their home while they were away and look after the family's beloved pet German shepherd.

On returning to work, Leik was informed that his nephew had in fact been previously interviewed regarding the slayings of several young women in the area. Feeling uneasy, Corporal Leik returned home and to the basement where he began to scrape away as much of the black paint as possible, moving the washing machine as he went. Beneath the paint he found brownish blood stains and, clumps of hair that matched his nephew. Gathering the hair samples in true forensic style, Leik returned to the police station and had the evidence sent for analysis.

The lab quickly confirmed that not only was the hair that of his nephew's, but also matched to the same hair samples found inside Karen's underwear.

The basement in Leiks home was immediately and thoroughly forensically tested. Detectives discovered bloodstains that matched Karen Beineman, confirming she had been in the basement. Additional evidence came from neighbours who recalled a young man fitting Collins description leaving his uncle's house carrying a large box of laundry and detergent. Another spoke of hearing muffled screams coming from the house on the night in question.

John Norman Collins was formally arrested on July the 30th 1969, for the murder and abduction of Karen Sue Beineman and was suspected of killing the other 6 victims in the Ypsilanti and Ann Arbour area between 1967 and1969.

In a twist of fate and with John Collin's DNA now clearly on file, he was soon charged for another unrelated murder. Roxie Ann Phillips, aged 17 years old from Monterey, California was found murdered in June 1969 -

just after the shocking brutal slaying of Alice Kalom, John Collin's 6th victim. Collins and his friends had taken a trip to Salinas, California at the time of Roxie's disappearance. Both physical and circumstantial evidence strongly linked Collins to her death and police pursued a 1st degree murder charge against him. Several motions would be filed by California to extradite Collins to stand trial, unfortunately and more bizarrely, all motions for his extradition were turned down. Collins' Defence Attorney, Neil Fink successfully opposed all such requests on the grounds of Due Process.

John Collin's trial was set for June the 2nd 1970 in the Washtenaw County Court in Ann Arbour. However, forensic evidence was slim and much of the sightings of Collins with his alleged victims, was at best, circumstantial. The prosecution team decided to only indict John on the murder of Beineman; his last victim given that detectives could at least present the hair evidence and matching blood sample they had discovered in Leik's basement.

This was to be a family forever torn apart.

Loretta Collins, who was her son's official spokesperson and continued to believe in his absolute innocence. Her blind love for her son tore her relationship apart with her sister and brother-in-law, the Leik family. She would never speak to them again.

It would take just twenty days for the locally selected jury from Ann Arbor to reach their verdict. John Colins was unanimously found guilty of 1st degree murder.

Before sentencing, the presiding judge, Judge Conlin asked the accused, John Collins if he would like to address the court. He replied 'Yes' and rose from his chair.

His cold yet confident statement echoed through the courtroom. "I have two things to say: I think the jury conscientiously tried to give me a fair trial. The jury did not take its task lightly, but I think things were blown out of proportion. The circumstances surrounding this case prevent me from getting a fair trial. Second, I never knew a girl named Karen sue Beineman; I never had a conversation with her. I never took her to a wig shop; I never took her to my uncles' home; I never took her life".

In 1972 California authorities dropped the extradition case against Collins, given that their suspect had now already received a life sentence and that much unnecessary resources would be tied up in giving the further victims of John Collins any justice. For them, it was clearly too much of a burden to take on.

Evidence however soon came to light that Roxie and Collins had been dating prior to her murder. She had confided in close friends that she was indeed dating an EMU student from Michigan by the name of John. She would also speak of his collection of motorcycles. But Roxie found no love. She found death through being strangled by her own pretty designer belt. Her body was found naked, stripped of dignity and dumped in a patch of poison oak on the 13^t of July. After Collins' original arrest, evidence of a red and white belt was found in a trailer he had owned during the time of her disappearance along with pubic hairs which were sent for analysis.

Despite the trauma, Roxie's family agreed to have her body exhumed in order for the necessary forensic comparisons to be made. The match was unrefutable.

Ironically Collins had at the time, sought hospital treatment for the adverse symptoms related to poison oak when he was in California and before he had returned home to Michigan that year.

Collins' mother Loretta, his brother Jerry and sister Gail continued to regularly visit him in Southern Michigan Prison, until in 1977 when he was transferred to Marquette Branch Prison. But there was no rehabilitation for John's mindset. With several mark ups for criminal activity and dealing in contraband in prison drugs, John was continually segregated from the rest of the prison population not only for his misdeeds, but ultimately for the safety of his inmates.

Collins continued to cause problems and in 1980, changed his surname to that of his biological father, Chapman, a Native Canadian. John's plan was to seek citizenship in Canada due to his dual nationality and in order to take advantage of their more lenient approach to sentencing. With the prospect of becoming a Canadian,

John could ultimately take advantage of their penal code where he could potentially be released after serving just nine years of his sentence instead of his whole natural life without a chance of parole.

The request was thankfully refused by the Court of Appeal who witnessed the absolute public disgust and outrage. Citizens had not forgotten John Collins' appalling crimes and the fact that he was only charged with one murder.

Loretta Collins sadly passed in 1983, still believing in her son's innocence. For her and both of John's siblings, a terrible miscarriage of justice had befallen him.

A new unbelievable turn of events was about to surface regarding the Collins case. In 2005 a former nurse by the name of Gary Earl Leiterman, aged 62 was to be charged with the murder of Jane Louise Mixer, Collins supposed 3rd victim. He was found guilty of her murder due to new DNA analysis evidence which was presented and not available at the time of the original murder or trial. Gary was convicted and sentenced to life imprisonment with no possibility of parole. The DNA of Gary had ultimately been found when Jane Louise Mixer's murder case was reopened in 2001. The jury would agree with the evidence of Leiterman's DNA being found on the victim's stockings.

At the time of the investigation, Gary Leiterman was never interviewed as a suspect at the time of the murder but, only lived twenty miles away from the University of

Michigan. Leiterman appealed his sentence but the Michigan court of appeals in 2007, upheld his guilty verdict and his life sentence charge.

One must be forced to reconsider Collins as a sole perpetrator. Did he act alone in these dark macabre acts of torture and sickening murders. Was it perhaps a type of sick sport which could involve others?

Collins himself states that he has knowledge of fellow fraternity brother's involvement but refuses to elaborate on his opportunity to a leaner sentence.

It is also alleged that one of the members of the Theta Chi brotherhood happens to also be one of John's Legal Advisors, who cannot be named.

John Normal Collins is known as the original co-ed killer as he prowled this earth before the likes of Ted Bundy's deadly tirade of death and sickening destruction. John still calls Maraguette State Prison home and is kept in a segregation unit under lock and key, for the rest of his natural life.

BIKINI KILLER

DAVID MORRISEY

There are few serial killers quite as successful as Charles Sobhraj. Fluent in several languages, extremely intelligent, and known for his irresistible charms with women, Sobhraj lived a life of nonstop thievery, murder, drugs, and scandal. His unstoppable resourcefulness allowed him to escape authorities half a dozen times through luck, timing, and even what seems to be a strange sense of fate. His favorite means of getting what he wanted involved befriending his victims through faked favors and gifts only to eventually drug and loot, or sometimes murder, them. Known as the "Bikini Killer", a name given to him after he brutally drowned two women and left their bodies dressed in similar bikinis, Charles Sobhraj stretched his crimes across an entire continent and three separate countries. Along the way, he gathered to himself many loyal followers, amassing a sort of cult-like group of acolytes that helped him scam, murder, and steal from nearly everyone he met. Narcissistic and carefree, Sobhraj never took being arrested and convicted of his crimes as a reason to stop. Instead, he routinely bribed guards and fellow inmates so that he could live his days in prison in the lap of luxury. He cheerfully recounts his actions to any news reporter or author that will give him the time of day, although he is careful never to say in so many words that he committed any murders. In addition to his more famous nickname, Sobhraj has also been dubbed "the Serpent". As of today, he has been convicted for only one of his believed 12-24 murders, and he is awaiting charges for a second.

This is the biography of serial killer and con artist Charles Sobhraj.

Charles Sobhraj's birth name was Hatchand Bhaonani Gurumukh Charles Sobrhaj. Born on April 6th, 1944 in Saigon, Vietnam, his mother was Vietnamese and his father was an Indian Sindhi. Unfortunately for Sobhraj, he was born into an unhappy family, as his mother and father were unmarried. Soon after his birth, his father abandoned Sobhraj and his mother to fend for themselves. Even when he was adopted by his mother's new boyfriend, a French Army lieutenant stationed in Indochina, any hope of a pleasant childhood quickly died. Neglected by his mother and adopted father in favor of the couple's later children, Sobhraj was bounced back and forth between France and Indochina with the family. Sobhraj hated his life, and as a child he attempted, at least twice, to escape his circumstances to Saigon from France by sea, reaching as far as Djibouti on one occasion. As a teenager, Sobhraj found an outlet for his frustrations through committing petty crimes. In 1963, he would be caught and convicted of burglary, serving his first prison sentence at Poissy prison, located near Paris. Sobhraj quickly realized that his charisma could be used in his favor and began manipulating prison officials into granting him special privileges, such as being allowed to keep books in his cell, enjoy extra free time, etc. At around this same point in time, he met and gained the favor of Felix d'Escogne, a wealthy young man and frequent prison volunteer.

Almost immediately after being paroled, Sobhraj moved in with d'Escogne and began sharing his time between moving in the high societal circles of Paris and the criminal underworld. Through a series of scams and burglaries, Sobhraj began amassing an impressive fortune. During this lucrative time, he met and began a passionate relationship with Chantal Compagnon, a young Parisian woman from a conservative family. Sobhraj asked for Compagnon's hand in marriage, but any happiness would be abruptly cut short as he was arrested the very same day for evading police while driving a stolen car. Compagnon remained supportive through his conviction and subsequent eight month prison sentence, however, and the two were married soon after his release.

In 1970 Sobhraj and then pregnant Chantal fled France for Asia and a new life, far from French jurisdiction. As they traveled through Eastern Europe with forged travel documents, the two robbed tourists whom they befriended along the way to keep their cash flow and opulent lifestyle moving smoothly. Eventually, the Sobhrajs arrived in Mumbai where Chantal gave birth to a baby girl, named Usha. In the meantime, Sobhraj happily reestablished his criminal lifestyle, running a car theft and smuggling operation. Money needed to be quickly gathered to fuel his blossoming gambling addiction.

His system worked well for a few years until he was arrested and imprisoned in 1973 for an unsuccessful armed robbery attempt on a jewelry store at Hotel Ashoka. Soon after, Sobhraj managed to escape with some help from his wife after faking an illness. Freedom was short lived, however, because they were quickly re-captured and returned to jail. This time, Sobhraj borrowed money for bail from his father and fled, taking his family to Kabul.

The family never slowed down, continuing their hobby of robbing tourists on what was called the "Hippie Trail", but they were eventually arrested once again. Not long after Sobhraj escaped a second time, even using the same method he had implemented in India: faking illness and drugging the hospital guard. This time around, Sobhraj fled to Iran, leaving his family behind to fend for themselves. Chantal, though still fiercely loyal to Sobhraj, returned to France and vowed to never see her husband again. After all the arrests, scams, and turmoil, Chantal had grown tired of a criminal lifestyle and sought to build a better life for herself and her young daughter.

Sobhraj spent the next two years on the run, using as many as ten stolen passports. Over time, Sobhraj passed through various countries in Eastern Europe and the Middle East, and he was eventually joined by his younger brother, Andre, in Istanbul. The two brothers quickly became partners in crime, committing crimes throughout both Turkey and Greece. The pair were eventually apprehended in Athens, but an escape plan that involved an identity switch failed, leading to the escape of only one brother, Sobhraj. Andre was eventually turned over to the Turkish police by Greek authorities and served his eighteen year sentence alone.

Forever on the run from the law, Sobhraj financed his opulent lifestyle by posing as both a gem salesman and drug dealer to impress and befriend tourists, whom he would then defraud. His travels took him to Thailand, where Sobhraj met Marie-Andree Leclerc from Levis, Quebec. Leclerc was a young tourist looking for adventure, and she mistakenly believed she had found it in the charismatic company of Sobhraj. Charmed by Sobhraj's magnetic personality, Leclerc quickly became a loyal follower, looking the other way when he committed crimes and ignoring his philandering ways with the local women.

Sobhraj soon began collecting more and more followers by winning their loyalty. He did this most often by helping his targets out of difficult situations. In one instance he helped two former French policemen, Yannick and Jacques, recover their missing passports. Unbeknownst to the two men, Sobhraj had in fact stolen their original passports. Another scheme had Sobhraj providing shelter to a Frenchman, named Domnique Rennelleau, who seemed to be suffering from an intense case of dysentery. The terrible truth was that Sobhraj had actually been poisoning Rennelleau. Finally, he was joined by a young Indian, named Ajay Chowdhury. Also a long practiced criminal, Chowdhury became Sobhraj's second-in-command, dutifully following Sobhraj's every grizzly order.

Sobhraj and Chowdhury's first recorded murders occurred in 1975. It was in the city of Pattaya, Thailand that this serial killer's story truly began. On a usual early morning, a fisherman in a long boat found the body of a young woman, known today to be Teresa Knowlton of Seattle, floating in the water. When the royal Thai police were alerted, they rushed to the scene. The coroner examined the victim and questioned the fishermen, but there was little to go on. They found no identification, and there were no signs of foul play. The coroner could only conclude that the woman was most likely a young Western tourist whose vacation had come to an abrupt and tragic end by a terrible swimming accident. At the morgue, the coroner routinely took down her fingerprints, and the woman's identity was listed as "unknown". A toxicology report revealed alcohol and hashish in her system, and the medical examiner had seen enough cases like this in his career to believe this was little more than a case of an unsuspecting tourist deciding to take a late night swim and falling prey to the water's dangerous rip tides, confirming the initial police report. Police then went about the routine business of uncovering the woman's identity, canvassing hotels near where her body was found, but they found nothing. While the investigation was under way, the police waited for a missing person report to fall across their desk, hoping to find the drowning victim's identity this way. For two months, nothing happened, until another discovery grabbed the attention of the Royal Thai police.

A worker driving his truck near the very same beach noticed something unusual in the brush that lined the road. It was the body of a second young Westerner. Police immediately combed the area, but they found few clues. She was a young woman, perhaps a student on an overseas vacation, but there was no identification with her body. There was no purse, wallet, or even a passport. In the beginning, there was little to no alarm raised over this. Reporter Alan Dawson covered the two deaths.

"People didn't really correlate for a while the appearance of one body and then another," said Dawson.

One person that did choose to pay attention was Somphol Suthimai, a lieutenant colonel in the Thai police department who was also the head of Interpol in Thailand. It was not the similarities between the cases that caught Suthimai's attention, but the differences.

"They were both found near the seaside, but the condition that the bodies were in was different," said Suthimai.

The police report stated that the second woman was deliberately drowned, and this conclusion cast an ominous shadow over the first victim's case. Perhaps she had been deliberately drowned as well.

"Thai officials have a problem. They have [two] dead bodies. They have no identification associated with them. They know they have an investigation that they have to pursue criminally, but one of the key steps to getting it started is the identification of the victims," said John Imhoff, director of Interpol's US office at the time.

To help identify the two women, pictures of the victims were released to the Bangkok Post. Tens of thousands in Southeast Asia started their day by reading this English-language newspaper, and police hoped that one of these readers could help them acquire a lead. Days later, however, the two women remained unidentified. Pattaya, Thailand, was hardly the place one would expect a killing spree. Known as the Riviera of Thailand, Pattaya catered to Westerners; young men and women looking for a good time in an exotic land.

"Young people were attracted to Thailand. They thought that it had so much to offer compared with their culture, and they would soak it all up. This would make them especially vulnerable to the predators who were on the Hippy Trail," said Dawson.

Less than a month after the two women were found in Pattaya, villagers found two more bodies. This time, it was a man and a woman. They were clearly young and again Western, and they were very clearly murdered.

"The bodies were still burning when they were discovered. This was a horrific crime," remarked Dawson.

Both victim's faces were badly burned, and police looked for anything that could help them identify the pair or give them some sort of lead to go on. All they were able to find was a tag on the woman's clothing that read "Made in Holland". The police still had no leads and no motive, and using forensic evidence, they reconstructed the murders.

"The woman was beaten with a hard object. The man was whipped, strangled, until he couldn't breathe," recounted Suthimai.

The coroner also found soot in both of the victim's air passages, indicating that the pair was still alive when they are set on fire. The Thai police searched everywhere for suspects and leads, but their efforts turned up nothing. Three women and one man, all between the ages of 18 and 25, were dead. Police hoped that information would come in along the tourist trail and prayed that somewhere someone had come across the murdered foreigners and picked up information that might result in a lead.

Meanwhile, news had yet to reach Katmandu, Nepal, which lies at the end of the Hippy Trail nearly 1400 miles away. At the time, both Nepal and Thailand had only recently joined Interpol, and their communication was rudimentary at best. Officials here had no idea a killer was on the move until two bodies were discovered outside of Katmandu. A pair of Nepalese boys stumbled across the grizzly scene, and it was a sight they would never forget, nor would the investigators. It was difficult to identify who the victims were, as the woman had a wound on her chest, and the man had a wound on his neck. Nepalese detective Bishwa Lal Shrestha was the lead detective for the case.

"When we saw the dead bodies, the faces were burned. They were naked. We had no idea who could have done this," said Shrestha.

Police turned the boys that had found the victims away after securing the crime scene. Such a gruesome image was not for young eyes. Police suspected the couple were traveling together, and in Katmandu there is one place they were sure to have gone: Jhhonchen Tole, also known as "Freak Street". Investigators began their search there in the hotels and hostels that catered to tourists. At one such establishment, the host remembered a couple that had gone backpacking and had not returned for several days. Their names were , Henk Bintanja, 29, and his fiancée Cornelia Hemker, 25. When police searched their room, they found most of their belongings still there, but their passports were gone. They also found a diary, and written inside was the name Alain Gautier, from Bangkok, Thailand. Friends of the pair that were staying next door told police everything they knew about the couple's last known activities. They claimed they remembered seeing Hemker with a man who claimed to be a gem dealer from Bangkok. Police asked the friends to identify the bodies, and they confirmed that the bodies belonged to their missing friends.

Six bodies had now been found, but the two police departments still were not in communication. It was up to Interpol to apprehend this serial killer. So far, police had no idea that they were chasing the same man: Charles Sobhraj.

"Charles can present a persona that is what the people want to see, not what he really is, so if he wants to assume a false identity he's practiced this for a long time," remarked Imhoff.

The woman killed in Nepal had been seen with a gem dealer named Allan Gautier, an alias used by Sobhraj. Throughout Katmandu, officers continued to search for leads. At one hotel they found a clerk who remembered a guest matching Sobhraj's description, but he was not registered under Allan Gautier. He was registered as a Dutch national by the name of Karl Gassel. The clerk informed police that Gassel drove a white car. Is was not much of a lead, but police searched all the same, setting up check points and checking dozens of cars. An officer pulled over a vehicle that matched the description, and the driver was calm as he produced passports, identifying himself as Karl Gassel. The woman, his wife, was Ida Bosch. Police called off the search and escorted the couple to the station for questioning. The man claimed to be a scholar and his wife a Dutch television star. He insisted he had never seen the victim before. When the witness was brought in to identify him, she could not positively identify him as the same man she saw with her friend.

The police let the couple go. The man they knew as Karl Gassel and his wife returned to their hotel. Days later, a Katmandu policeman took a statement from a witness who saw a white car near where the bodies were found. Somehow, she even remembered the license plate number, which matched the plate on Gassel's car. Then came the hard evidence. Police found two arrival cards for the victim Pierre Beaumont, and the two signatures did not match. A handwriting expert found that aspects of the second signature were very similar to those of Gassel's. The second arrival card was also dated December the 24th, the same day Pierre Beaumont's corpse was brought in to the coroner's office. Police concluded that the man called Karl Gassel had left the country and returned using the dead man's passport. Now with a case against Gassel, police hurried to make an arrest. It was too late. Sobhraj and his companion were long gone. There were clothes, documents, tools for amending passports, and gasoline were found in the couple's apartment. It would be months before the information of Sobhraj and his escape reached Interpol.

"You can wait two days to get a call through to Nepal, and communications are not what they are now at all. By the time authorities could really make a case it was quite some time down the road and he was long gone," said Dawson.

In Thailand, there were still no suspects, and no identities for the four murdered Western tourists. They still had no idea that there are two additional victims in Nepal. Nothing like this had happened before, and police were investigating the possibility that the perpetrator was a Thai resident. While Thai police were hard at work, the Dutch embassy in Bangkok received a vital clue. Herman Knippenberg, a diplomat there, received a letter about a missing Dutch couple that had been vacationing in Thailand.

"I was very worried about the fact that for a period of over six weeks they had not had a sign of life from the couple," said Knippenberg.

Knippenberg had no idea at the time how important the couple's names would become. The names were Karl Gassel and Ida Bosch. In the missing couple's last letter they wrote that they had made a sophisticated new friend in Bangkok. The man was a gem dealer, and he was helping the pair buy and sell precious stones. The man had taken them to dinner and invited them to his apartment for drinks. That letter would be the last any of their families heard of their loved ones, Karl and Ida. Desperate and unable to help with their own power, family members asked Interpol's office in Thailand to help find their missing love ones. Knippenberg contacted Thai authorities and gave them the names of the two missing tourists, but the Thai police had no information about the missing couple. By communicating with the Australian office, Knippenberg learned of an Australian couple that were drugged and robbed by a gem dealer. This gem dealer ran by the name Alain Gautier. Sobhraj is a man capable of casting false lead after false lead, using his aliases to throw Interpol and local police off his trail for as long as he needs. By the time authorities discovered one of his aliases, he was long gone again, leaving victims dead or robbed in his wake. Such was the case with Alain Gautier the gem dealer.

Sobhraj's next victim was a nomadic Sephardic Jew by the name of Vitali Hakim, whose body was found on the side of a road leading to the Pattaya resort, where Sobhraj and his growing group of followers were staying. The young man's body was found with his neck snapped and partially burned with gasoline. Two Dutch students, Henk Bintanja, 29, and his fiancée Cornelia Hemker, 25, were invited to Thailand after meeting Sobhraj in Hong Kong. Following his usual scam, Sobhraj poisoned the young couple before nurturing them back to health and gaining their blind loyalty. As the pair were recovering, Sobhraj had a surprise visitor: the French girlfriend of Vitali Hakim, Charmayne Carrou, who had come demanding answers about her lover's sudden disappearance. Fearful of being exposed, Sobhraj and his murderous partner Chowdhury quickly moved to deal with the Dutch students that had heard too much. On December 16th, 1975, their damaged bodies were found strangled and burned. Soon after, poor Carrou was found drowned and wearing a bikini that was eerily similar to that which Teresa Knowlton had been found wearing. It would be months of fruitless searching and investigating before either women would be identified. It would be even longer before the two murders were connected, but Sobhraj would eventually be given the ominous nickname, "Bikini Killer".

On December 18th, the day the burned bodies of Bintanja and Hemker were identified, Sobhraj and Leclerc entered Nepal using the murdered pair's passports. After meeting in up inside the country on what investigators believe was either the 21st or 22nd of December, Sobhraj and Leclerc murdered Laurent Carriere, a 26-year-old from Canada, and Connie Bronzich, a 29-year-old from the United States. Some sources misidentified the pair as Laddie DuParr and Annabella Tremont. After their deaths, Sobhraj and Leclerc returned to Thailand, using Bintanja and Hemker's stolen passports before authorities could put anyone on alert for the missing documents. Upon his return, Sobhraj realized that his three French followers had begun to suspect him of his murders, having discovered his hidden stash of stolen documents belonging to the murder victims. The three notified authorities and fled for their lives back to Paris, convinced that Sobhraj would move to kill them for knowing too much.

Sobhraj next found himself in Calcutta, on the run as usual, where he killed Israeli professor Avoni Jacob. Investigators believe that Sobhraj committed the murder simply to acquire the victim's passport. Sobhraj used the stolen document to travel with Leclerc and Chowdhury. The small group hopped from Singapore, to India, and finally, back to Bangkok in March of 1976. They were quickly caught and given lengthy interrogations by Thai policemen regarding their possible connection to the murders, but they were eventually released because authorities feared the negative publicity that a murder trial would bring might harm the country's tourist industry.

At the same time, Dutch official Herman Knippenberg was still hot on the trail, investigating into the murders of Bintanja and Hemker. Knippenberg knew a little of, and had allegedly even met, Sobhraj, but his real name had not been obtained at that time and Sobhraj managed to slip out of Knippenberg's fingers. Knippenberg tirelessly gathered evidence, and, with the cooperation of Sobhraj's neighbor, slowly but surely built a case against him. Knippenberg eventually won permission from police to search Sobhraj's apartment, but this search did not occur until a full month after Sobhraj had left the country. In spite of this, Knippenberg was able to obtain a substantial amount of evidence, ranging from Sobhraj's victim's stolen documents and passports to poisons and syringes. Meanwhile, the three serial criminals stopped in Malaysia, where Chowdhury was sent to steal gems for a gem salesman scam. Chowdhury was seen delivering the gems to Sobhraj, but this would prove to be the last time Sobhraj's longtime partner would be seen alive. Neither Chowdhury nor his remains were ever found, and it is believed by investigators that Sobhraj murdered his former partner before leaving Malaysia. Leclerc and Sobhraj then moved to Geneva in order to sell the stolen gems as gem salesmen. Although Chowdhury was allegedly spotted in Germany, the claim has gone unsubstantiated, and the search for Chowdhury, alive or dead, continues.

Soon after returning to Asia, Sobhraj started to rebuild a new "family" of devoted followers, starting with two lost Western women, Barbara Smith and Mary Ellen Eather, in Bombay. Sobhraj's next believed victim was a Frenchman by the name of Jean-Luc Solomon, who he accidentally killed with poison. It is believed that in this case, Sobhraj intended merely to incapacitate the man so that he could be robbed. Sometime in July of 1976, Sobhraj, joined in New Delhi by his three female companions in crime, tricked a tour group of French post-graduate students into accepting them as tour guides. Sobhraj drugged the group, giving them poison laced pills that he told them were anti-dysentery medicine. The drugs acted more quickly than Sobhraj had estimated, however, and the students began losing consciousness. Seeing their comrades fall victim to the pills, the few that remained conscious realized what Sobhraj had done, overpowered him, and contacted police. This brave act finally lead to this career criminal and serial murderer's capture. Barbara and Mary Ellen quickly broke during interrogation and confessed to their involvement with

Sobhraj and his long list of crimes. Sobhraj was charged with the murder of Solomon, and all four were sent to Tihar prison, New Delhi, where they awaited trial. To Sobhraj, however, this was an experience he had had many times.

Barbara and Mary Ellen could not bear to face the consequences of their actions, and in the two years leading up to their trial each attempted suicide. On the other hand, an always prepared Sobhraj had smuggled precious gems into prison by hiding them within his body, and he immediately began bribing guards in order to live comfortably within the jail. Sobhraj quickly turned his trial into a one man show, hiring and firing lawyers without hesitation, bringing in his newly paroled brother Andre to assist, and even going so far as to go on a hunger strike. Although he was expected to receive the death penalty, a shocking conviction gave him only twelve years. It would seem this charismatic psychopath could not be touched. Leclerc was found guilty of the drugging of the French students, was eventually paroled, and returned to Canada. Her crime spree stopped there, as she developed ovarian cancer. She swore her innocence and remained dutifully loyal to Sobhraj until the day she died in her home in April of 1984.

Meanwhile, Sobhraj's constant bribery of prison guards at Tihar prison had reached incredible levels. He led a life of opulence and luxury within the jail, with his own TV and frequent gourmet food. His gregarious and persuasive personality had earned him key friendships with guards and fellow prisoners. His arrogance did not stop there, as he routinely gave interviews to Western authors and journalists, such as Oz magazine's Richard Neville in the late 1970s and Alan Dawson in 1984. He happily talked about his murders while never openly admitting to them, and he pretended that his choices were fueled by a hatred for Western imperialism in Asia. Sometime after Neville's book *The Life and Crimes of Charles Sobhraj* came out, a work based entirely on an extended taped conversation Sobhraj had with Neville, Sobhraj denied everything he had said to the reporter.

Even with all his built up luxuries, Sobhraj had a problem facing him at the end of his twelve year sentence. The arrest warrant he had acquired in Thailand would still be valid, meaning he would be extracted to Thailand and almost certainly executed. To avoid this inevitable doom, in March of 1986, Sobhraj threw an enormous party for his guards and fellow inmates, drugged them with large doses of sleeping pills, and simply walked out of jail after serving ten of his twelve years. It would not be long before inspector Madhukar Zende of the Mumbai police found and recaptured Sobhraj in O'Coquero Restaurant in Goa. His prison term was immediately increased by an additional ten years for his escape, but this was exactly what Sobhraj had hoped for. On the 17th of February, 1997, a 52-year-old Sobhraj was released with almost all of his warrants, case evidence, and even witnesses that would have put him away long lost or invalid. Without a country to extradite the murderer to, Indian authorities had no choice but to allow him to return to France.

Late into 2007, it was reported that Sobhraj's lawyer had appealed to the current French president, Nicolas Sarkozy, for intervention with Nepal. By 2008, Sobhraj had announced his new engagement to a Nepali woman by the name of Nihita Diswas. On the 7th of July, 2008, Sobhraj issued a press released through his fiancée Nihita, claiming that since he was never convicted of murder by a jury, the media should stop referring to him as a serial killer. It sparked a lot of controversy, and once again his face was plastered on news channels across the world.

Some believed that he married his fiancée on October 9th, 2008, while in jail on Bada Dashami, a Nepalese festival, but the claims were dismissed by jail authorities the following day. They did confirm, however, that Nihita and her family were allowed into the prison to conduct a tika ceremony along with the relatives of hundreds of other prisoners. They insisted that this was not a wedding at all but just a part of the ongoing Dashain festival, where elders place the vermilion mark on the foreheads of those younger than them to signify their blessings.

In July of 2010, The Supreme Court of Nepal delayed the verdict on an appeal served by Sobhraj against a district court's judgment which sent him to life in prison for the killing of American tourist Connie Bronzich in 1975. Sobhraj had appealed against the verdict in 2006, claiming that the verdict had been an unfair act of racism from the judges. On July 30th, 2010, the Nepalese Supreme Court moved to uphold the verdict issued by the district court, adding an additional year and a 2000Rs fine for using a fake passport to travel. The court further mandated the immediate seizure of all his properties. His mother-in-law, who was also his lawyer, Shakuntala Thapa, and his "wife" Nihita expressed unhappiness with the verdict, and Thapa claimed that Sobhraj had been denied justice and that the judiciary was corrupt. The two were detained and sent into judicial custody for contempt of court because of these opinionated remarks. Sobhraj may never have been caught in Nepal at all, had it not been for a journalist who happened to recognize him in Katmandu in 2003. It was this twist of fate that had him arrested for his murder of Bronzich and Carriere decades before. When arrested, it is reported that he denied ever having been to Nepal before and that he was there to make a TV documentary.

Sobhraj is currently awaiting another trial for a case against him in the Bhaktapur district court for the murder of Canadian tourist Laurent Carriere. As of September 2014, Sobraj was convicted in Nepal of another murder.

TED BUNDY

KENNETH PUTNAM

Ted Bundy is one of the most prolific serial killers of the 20th century, having kidnapped, raped, and murdered at least 36 attractive young women between 1973 and 1978 in Colorado, Oregon, Utah, Florida, and Washington; however, many assert that this figure could be much higher. He had also kept some of his victims' body parts—including heads—as trophies in a utility shed behind his Utah home, as well having engaged in necrophilia with decomposing corpses which he would groom and apply makeup.

A master manipulator and classic antisocial personality, Bundy escaped custody twice; once from court during his first murder trial and the second time from the Garfield County Jail in Colorado by sawing a hole in his cell ceiling. He was placed on the FBI's Ten Most Wanted list and was later arrested in Florida in February 1978 after stealing a car. He was sentenced to death in 1979 for the murder of two Florida State University sorority sisters, and again in 1980 for another murder.

Very charismatic and handsome, Bundy exploited these characteristics heavily with his young female victims in an effort to earn their sympathy trust. He would often approach potential victims in public places, feigning injury or impersonating an authority figure before overpowering them—usually by hitting them in the head with a crowbar—taking them to secluded locations, and raping and murdering them. Sometimes he would simply break into young women's homes and bludgeon them while they slept.

Bundy was originally incarcerated for aggravated kidnapping and attempted assault in 1975 in Utah; however, his list of homicide victims continued to grow. He escaped from custody twice in Colorado and subsequently committed three more murders before finally being apprehended in Florida in 1978. Ted Bundy was sentenced to death and was executed in the electric chair at Raiford Prison in Starke, Florida, on 24 January 1989.

Early Life

Theodore Robert Bundy—originally Theodore Robert Cowell—was born on 24 November 1946 at the Elizabeth Lund Home for Unwed Mothers in Burlington, Vermont. The social stigma of being a single mother was great at that time so Bundy's mother, Louise Cowell, took her infant son to live with her parents—Samuel and Eleanor—in Philadelphia where young Ted took on the Cowell surname and was told that they were, in fact, his parents and that his mother was his sister. Eventually, Bundy discovered the truth and harbored lifelong resentment toward his mother for lying to him.

Bundy's paternity has never been definitively proven. His birth certificate lists his father as Lloyd Marshall, an Air Force veteran and salesman; however, Louise has claimed that she was "seduced by 'a sailor'" whose name "may have been Jack Worthington" but nobody by that name was ever found in Navy or merchant marines records. Compounding the problem is that Bundy's grandfather, Samuel Cowell, has been rumored to be his biological father; thus making Bundy the product of incest; however, again, there is no evidence of this.

In interviews, Bundy spoke highly of his grandparents, especially expressing a fondness for his grandfather even though other family members described Samuel as a tyrannical bully and bigot who beat his wife and dog, abused his daughters, harmed neighborhood cats, and would sometimes "speak aloud to unseen presences". Bundy's grandmother was timid and obedient and was treated for her depression with electroconvulsive therapy.

Bundy exhibited disturbing behavior from a young age. At the age of three, he was alleged to have surrounded his sleeping aunt, Julia, with household knives—blades pointed toward her—and smiled at her when she had awakened.

In 1950, when Bundy was only four, Louise changed both her and her son's surname to Nelson and moved them both to Tacoma, Washington, to live with cousins Jane and Alan Scott. In 1951, Louise met hospital cook Johnny Culpepper Bundy at a church singles night and they married later that year. Johnny formally adopted young Ted and he adopted the last name of Bundy. Even with efforts to include young Ted in family activities along with his four half-siblings—who he was often left to babysit—he always was distant. Later, Bundy would tell his girlfriend that Johnny wasn't his real dad, wasn't smart enough, and didn't make much money.

Bundy confessed that he "chose to be alone" as an adolescent and neither had any natural inclination to develop any close friendships nor knew what drove people to be friends in the first place. He would later say that he "hit a wall" and his inability to comprehend social behavior stunted his social development, rendering him required to adopt a façade of social activity. He was terribly shy, self-doubting, and uncomfortable in social situations and often teased for being different. Despite this, he was a good student at Woodrow Wilson High School, was active in a local Methodist church, and was even involved with a local Boy Scout troop.

Bundy would also admit—while on death row—that a part of him as a young child was "fascinated by images of sex and violence" and he called this part "the entity". He enjoyed reading crime books and detective magazines, particularly those that contained descriptions of sexual violence and pictures of dead bodies. Later, before his execution, he would admit that pornography was central in shaping who he was.

Throughout high school Bundy loved to ski and was very good at it; however, his pursuit of this hobby was usually accomplished with stolen equipment and forged lift tickets. He was also arrested on at least two occasions on suspicion of auto theft and burglary but when he turned 18 his juvenile record was expunged. Stealing, for Bundy, did not involve any guilt and, in fact, he had a sense of entitlement about the entire thing. He often said that the thrill of taking possession of something he wanted without remorse was exciting. Many speculate that his "taking" of his victims represented this same concept and provided him with the same rush. Compounding the problem was his sense of entitlement and cunning ability to lie about everything which demonstrates a common trait among psychopaths.

Bundy graduated high school in 1965 and was awarded a scholarship by the University of Puget Sound where he started that fall, taking courses in Oriental studies and psychology. After two semesters he transferred to the University of Washington in Seattle.

He obtained employment as a stock boy and bagger at a Safeway store on Queen Anne Hill, in addition to other odd jobs. As part of his psychology curricula, he would work as a night-shift volunteer at Seattle's Suicide Hot Line where he met and worked Ann Rule who would later become among the world's foremost true crime writers and who penned a biography about Bundy—that was also partly autobiographical about her working relationship with him—entitled *The Stranger Beside Me* (1980).

While in college, circa 1968, Bundy began a relationship with fellow student "Stephanie Brooks" (a pseudonym); however, after she graduated in 1968 and prepared to move back home to California she broke up with Bundy due to what she described as his lack of ambition and immaturity. Bundy was heartbroken after this and, interestingly, all of his victims bore some resemblance to Brooks; particularly the fact that Brooks and all of his victims had long dark hair which they wore parted down the middle.

Shortly thereafter, Bundy returned to Burlington—his birthplace—and learned the truth of his parentage. This discovery made him more dominant and focused.

He managed the Seattle office of Nelson Rockefeller's presidential campaign in 1968 and attended the 1968 Republican convention in Miami, Florida. He reenrolled at the University of Washington with a major in psychology. He became popular among his professors as he was an honor student and also began a relationship with Elizabeth Kloepfer in 1969. Kloepfer was a divorced secretary with a young daughter and the two dated for the next six years until he went to prison in 1976.

Bundy graduated in 1972 with a degree in psychology and went to work for the state Republican Party.

In the fall of 1973, Bundy enrolled in the University of Utah Law School but did poorly because of poor attendance and, consequently, dropped out the following spring.

While in California on a business trip in the summer of 1973, Bundy found his ex-girlfriend "Stephanie Brooks" and the change in his look and attitude was appealing to her. Bundy courted Brooks the rest of the year—while still involved with Kloepfer—and proposed to her, only to dump Brooks shortly after the new year, likely in retaliation for her breaking his heart years earlier. The breakup wreaked havoc on Bundy who became obsessed with her and this obsession "would span his lifetime and lead to a series of events that would shock the world".

Mere weeks later, Bundy began his first murderous rampage in Washington; however, many Bundy experts assert that he likely starting killing in his teens. One case involved eight-year-old Ann Marie Burr from Tacoma who disappeared from her home in 1961 when Bundy was 14. Burr's house was on Bundy's newspaper delivery route and her father was positive that he saw Bundy near a construction site ditch on the nearby University of Puget Sound campus the day his daughter vanished. Despite other potentially incriminating circumstantial evidence, Bundy remains merely a suspect due to a lack of consensus by law enforcement personnel as to whether they believe he actually did it or not. Bundy has always denied killing her.

Shortly before his execution, Bundy did, in fact, tell his attorney that his first attempt at kidnapping was in 1969 and his first "actual murder" occurred "sometime in 1972". While he was a suspect in the December 1973 murder of Kathy Devine in Washington, DNA analysis exonerated him and her true murderer was convicted in 2002.

Bundy's earliest identified murders were committed in 1974 when he was 27.

Bundy was a handsome and charismatic guy, particularly to his young female victims and he exploited these characteristics fully. He was also an adept chameleon, able to blend in and feign belonging which increased his threat to the attractive brunette women he targeted as his victims. This charm and his adroitness at lying and manipulation made him extremely dangerous.

Known Murder Victims

Karen Sparks (often referred to as Joni Lenz), 18 (survived)

On 4 January 1974, 18-year-old Karen Sparks/Joni Lenz was found by her roommates when she didn't emerge from her bedroom that morning. They were not prepared for what horrific sights they saw. Sparks had been beaten badly and a bed rod ripped from the bed was "savagely rammed into her vagina". Sparks was transported to the hospital in a coma and suffered damages which continue to plague her.

However, she was one of the lucky few victims to survive an attack by Bundy.

Lynda Ann Healy, 21

A very accomplished and beautiful young woman, 21-year-old Lynda Healy announced ski conditions for all of the western Washington resorts on the radio. A senior at the University of Washington, she came from a good family, loved to sing, and was majoring in psychology. She shared a house with four other young women near the university. On 31 January, Healy and some friends went to a tavern and then home to bed. Her roommate in the next room never heard any sounds emanating from Healy's room that night.

The following morning when she didn't emerge from her bedroom after her alarm clock sounded at its usual 5:30 a.m. to go to work—and her job called looking for her—her roommate noticed that her bed was made in a peculiar way. Further inspection showed that the top sheet and a pillowcase were missing, a small bloodstain that was the same type as Lynda's was on the pillow and the bottom sheet, and a bloody nightgown was hanging in her closet. One of her outfits was missing. Also worrisome was that one of the doors was unlocked.

Initially, due to the absence of fingerprint, hair, or fiber evidence, police did not suspect foul play; however, later, they did come to realize that an intruder came in, removed Healy's nightgown and dressed her in another outfit, made the bed, wrapped her up, and took her out of the house.

Donna Gail Manson, 19

On 12 March, in Olympia, 19-year-old Evergreen State College student Donna Manson was kidnapped and murdered.

Susan Elaine Rancourt, 18

On 17 April, Susan Rancourt, 18, disappeared from the Central Washington State College campus in Ellensburg while walking across campus, alone, at night.

Later, two other female coeds would report meeting a good-looking man with his arm in a cast—one the night Rancourt disappeared and one three nights earlier—who asked for assistance with carrying books to his VW Beetle.

Roberta Kathleen "Kathy" Parks, 22

Kathy Parks, 22, was last seen on 6 May on the Oregon State University campus in Corvallis en route to meeting friends for coffee.

Brenda Carol Ball, 22

22-year-old Brenda Ball was last seen leaving the Flame Tavern in Burien, Oregon on 1 June.

Georgeann Hawkins, 18

In the early morning hours of 11 June, University of Washington student and a member of Kappa Alpha Theta Georgeann Hawkins, 18, left her boyfriend's dormitory en route to her sorority house through an alley. She was never seen again; however, witnesses later stated they had seen a man with a leg cast struggling to carry a briefcase in that area. Another female coed reported that he had asked her for help in carrying his briefcase to his VW Beetle.

Bundy later confessed to having lured Hawkins to his car, clubbed her with a tire iron he had hidden underneath his vehicle, and then took her elsewhere to rape and strangle her to death.

Janice Ann Ott, 23, and Denise Marie Naslund, 19

On 14 July, Janet Ott, 23, and Denise Naslund, 19, were abducted mere hours apart from Lake Sammamish State Park in Issaquah, Washington, in broad daylight. On that day, eight different witnesses reported seeing a handsome young man with his arm in a sling who called himself "Ted" and who asked several women for help unloading a sailboat from his VW Beetle. One witness said she walked with him for a ways but didn't see a sailboat and then declined to help him. Other witnesses stated that they saw the man approach Ott and she was observed walking away with him.

Naslund disappeared four hours later.

At this point, police in King County put up fliers with the suspected murderer's description all over the Seattle area. One of Bundy's psychology professors, former coworker Ann Rule, and Bundy's girlfriend Elizabeth Kloepfer reported him as a possible suspect. In fact, Kloepfer (who since changed her surname to Kendall and penned a book called *The Phantom Prince: My Life with Ted Bundy* in 1981) told the Seattle Police Department that her boyfriend "might be involved" in the recent Seattle murders. She called again later that autumn with more information and agreed to give them recent pictures of Bundy to be shown to witnesses; however, many of them could not positively identify him.

Ott's and Naslund's remains were found on 7 September off Interstate 90 near Issaquah, only one mile from the park where they were abducted. Near the women's remains was an extra femur and vertebrae which Bundy confessed before his execution belonged to Hawkins.

Between 1 March and 3 March 1975, the skulls and jawbones belonging to Healy, Rancourt, Parks, and Ball were found just east of Issaquah on Taylor Mountain. Bundy confessed in his death row interview that he kept the decapitated heads of these four victims in his apartment for some time and that he would revisit this dump site often to engage in sex with the corpses until decomposition became too great to continue. Bundy also admitted that he dumped Manson's body there as well—but burned her skull in his girlfriend's fireplace—however, no trace of her was ever recovered.

Other trophies discovered when Bundy's apartment was searched include photographs of his victims and a large bag of women's clothing.

Nancy Wilcox, 16

Bundy began the University of Utah Law School in the autumn of 1974. On 2 October 1974, 16-year-old Nancy Wilcox disappeared from Holladay, Utah. She was last seen in a VW Beetle.

Melissa Smith, 17

On 18 October, 17-year-old Melissa Smith—the daughter of Midvale, Utah's Police Chief Louis Smith—disappeared after leaving a pizza parlor. Nine days later she was found strangled, raped, and sodomized.

Laura Aime, 17

17-year-old Laura Aime disappeared from a Halloween party in Lehi, Utah. Her naked corpse was found on Thanksgiving Day by hikers near a river in the Wasatch Mountains. She had been beaten about the head and face with a crowbar and was raped and sodomized. The lack of blood at the crime scene indicated that she was likely killed elsewhere and dumped in this location. Police found no other physical evidence.

Carol DaRonch, 18 (survived)

On 8 November, 18-year-old Carol DaRonch was shopping at the Fashion Place Mall in Salt Lake City, Utah, and was approached by a man in the Sears parking lot who claimed to be a police officer named Officer Roseland. He told her that her car had been stolen and that he would take her to the police station to retrieve it. He took her to his VW Beetle and she became suspicious and asked him for identification. He quickly flashed a gold badge and she got in but refused his order to fasten her seat belt. After a short distance, Bundy pulled over and attempted to place handcuffs on DaRonch but only managed one wrist. He also attempted to hit her with a crowbar which she was able to catch before it hit her head. DaRonch fought back, kicking him in the groin, and as the car was speeding away she jumped out of it.

DaRonch flagged down another car and they took her to the police who confirmed there was no Officer Roseland. Police were able to obtain a description of the assailant and his car and a blood sample from DaRonch's coat. Type O; the same as Bundy's.

Debra Kent, 17

Mere hours after losing DaRonch Bundy abducted 17-year-old Debra "Debi" Kent from the parking lot of a school in Bountiful, Utah, as she was leaving a school play. She had told her parents she was going to pick up her brother at the bowling alley and she would be back to pick them up soon but never returned. She didn't even make it to her car which was still in the parking lot. Police found a small handcuff key in the parking lot and when they tried the key in the handcuffs DaRonch was wearing, it was a perfect fit.

A month later a man called the police and told them that he saw a tan VW Beetle speeding away from the high school parking lot the night Kent disappeared.

Shortly before he was to be executed, Bundy confessed that he dumped Kent's body near Fairview, Utah. After an intense search of the area, a human kneecap which was consistent with someone of Kent's age and size was found; however, DNA analysis was not conducted.

Caryn Campbell, 23

Bundy's first murder of 1975 occurred on 12 January. 23-year-old Michigan nurse Caryn Campbell disappeared between her hotel's lounge and her room while on a ski trip with her fiancé, Dr. Raymond Gadowski, and his two children, in Snowmass, Colorado. Frantic Gadowski called the police the next morning but a search proved futile.

Nearly a month later—and only a few short miles from where she went missing—a recreational worker discovered Campbell's nude body near the road. Animal damage to her body made it difficult to determine the exact cause of death; however, there was evidence of repeated, crushing blows to her head by a sharp instrument. Some of the blows were so violent that one of her teeth separated from the gums.

Julie Cunningham, 26

On 15 March, 26-year-old Vail ski instructor Julie Cunningham disappeared on her way to a nearby tavern. Bundy confessed in prison that he used his crutches ploy to approach Cunningham to ask for her help carrying ski boots to his car before he clubbed her with his crowbar, handcuffed her, and took her to a secluded location where strangled her.

Denise Oliverson, 25

25-year-old Denise Oliverson vanished in Grand Junction on 6 April while riding her bicycle to visit her parents.

Lynette Culver, 13

13-year-old Lynette Culver was abducted from her school playground at Alameda Junior High School in Pocatello, Idaho.

Susan Curtis, 15

Once Bundy returned to Utah, 15-year-old Susan Curtis vanished on 28 June while walking alone to the Brigham Young University dormitories during a youth conference she was attending. Bundy confessed to her murder minutes before his execution.

The bodies of Cunningham, Oliverson, Culver, and Curtis have never been found.

First Arrest, Trial, and Escapes

Bundy was first arrested on 16 August 1975 in Salt Lake City for failure to stop his vehicle for police. A search of his car unearthed a crowbar, handcuffs, ski mask, trash bags, an icepick, and other items the officer thought were burglary tools. The always calm and collected Bundy explained reasons why he had the items such as that he used the mask for skiing and had found the handcuffs in a dumpster; however, Detective Jerry Thompson connected Bundy and his Volkswagen to the DaRonch kidnapping and other missing girls and searched his apartment.

The search yielded a brochure of Colorado ski resorts with a checkmark by where Campbell had disappeared. Bundy was brought in for a lineup before DaRonch and other witnesses at the time DaRonch was kidnapped and they all identified him as Officer Roseland, as well as the man lurking about on the night Debbie Kent vanished.

After a week-long trial, Bundy was convicted on 1 March 1976 of kidnapping DaRonch and was sentenced to 15 years in Utah State Prison. Bundy was then extradited to Colorado to stand trial for murder.

He was able to escape custody twice before his eventual final arrest in Florida. The first escape occurred on 7 June 1977, when he was transported from the Garfield County Jail in Glenwood Springs, Colorado, to Pitkin County Courthouse in Aspen for his preliminary hearing. As he was serving as his own attorney, the judge excused him from being handcuffed and shackled. During a recess Bundy asked if he could research his case in the courthouse's law library. Hiding behind a bookcase he jumped from a second-story window, spraining his ankle when he landed. After shedding his suit, he simply walked through the town of Aspen as roadblocks were being erected before hiking southward on Aspen Mountain.

Near its summit he burglarized a cabin and stole clothing, food, and a rifle before heading toward Crested Butte; however, Bundy became lost and ended up wandering aimlessly for two days before breaking into a camping trailer on Maroon Lake where he took more food and a parka. Bundy then walked back toward Aspen and stole a car parked at the Aspen Golf Course. Two police officers noticed him weaving in traffic and pulled over the six-day fugitive. In the car were maps of the mountains around Aspen that the prosecutor was using to demonstrate where victim Caryn Campbell's body was found. As Bundy was his own attorney, he had the right of discovery to this evidence, thus demonstrating that he had planned his escape.

Bundy's second escape occurred on 30 December 1977, after having his motion for a change of venue to Denver accepted but with the venue being Colorado Springs instead; a city that had historically been hostile to murder suspects. He had managed to acquire the jail's floor plan and a hacksaw blade from other inmates, as well as $500 in cash smuggled in over a six-month period by visitors—particularly one Carole Ann Boone. In the evening while other inmates were showering, Bundy sawed a one-foot-square hole in his cell's ceiling—behind the steel bars—and was able to fit through it into the crawlspace above after losing 35 pounds. Prior to his actual escape, Bundy "practiced" and multiple reports of possible movement in the ceiling's crawlspace were, curiously, never investigated.

On the night of his escape, Bundy piled files and books under his covers in his bunk to look like his sleeping body, climbed into the crawlspace, broke through the jail's ceiling which, incidentally, was the chief jailer's apartment who just happened to be out for the evening with his wife. Bundy stole some street clothes and casually sauntered out the front door.

Bundy stole a car and drove east; however, the car broke down on Colorado's Interstate 70. A passing motorist gave him a ride into Vail where he caught a bus to Denver and then took a flight to Chicago, Illinois. From there he took an Amtrak train to Ann Arbor, Michigan.

His escape was discovered over 17 hours after the fact at noon on New Year's Eve.

Lisa Levy, 20, Margaret Bowman, 21, Karen Chandler (survived), Kathy Kleiner Deshields (survived)

On 15 January 1978—after Bundy had escaped from jail in Colorado, he traveled to Tallahassee, Florida, and attacked Chi Omega sorority sisters at Florida State University. At approximately 3:00 a.m. he entered the sorority house where he raped and strangled 20-year-old Lisa Levy to death; bludgeoned 21-year-old Margaret Bowman to death; and also bludgeoned Karen Chandler and Kathy Kleiner—both of whom survived.

The entire rampage took only 30 minutes.

Cheryl Thomas (survived)

That same morning, a mere eight blocks from the Chi Omega sorority house, Bundy attacked Cheryl Thomas in her bed and bludgeoned her with a wooden club, severely injuring her.

Kimberly Leach, 12

On 9 February, Bundy kidnapped 12-year-old Kimberly Leach from her junior high school in Lake City, Florida. Her raped, murdered, and dumped body was found in Suwannee River State Park underneath a small pig shed.

Bundy then stole another VW Beetle and left Tallahassee, traveling west across the Florida panhandle.

Florida Arrest

On 15 February 1978 shortly after 1:00 a.m., Bundy was stopped by Pensacola police officer David Lee who learned that the vehicle was stolen. After a brief scuffle, Lee had subdued and restrained Bundy and then took him to jail. During the transport, Bundy allegedly told Lee that he wished the officer would have killed him. Once his identity was confirmed, Bundy was transported to Tallahassee and charged with the Tallahassee and Lake City murders.

Florida Trials and Convictions

Among the most damning evidence during Bundy's June 1979 Chi Omega murder trial were bite marks found on Lisa Levy's left buttock which matched a plaster cast taken from Bundy's mouth. Additionally, Chi Omega sister Nita Neary was returning home late that night and saw Bundy as he left. She was able to identify him in court.

Bundy was convicted on all counts and sentenced to death.

In 1980, Bundy stood trial for the Kimberly Leach murder. Again, he was convicted, this time based upon fiber evidence and an eyewitness who saw him leading Leach away from the school. Bundy was, again, sentenced to death.

After his sentences he sought a stay of execution or commutation of his death sentences to life imprisonment by having one of his legal advocates contact his victims' families to ask them to ask for mercy in order to find out where their loved ones' remains were. This ploy for more time failed.

Execution

Bundy ultimately met his demise in Raiford Prison's electric chair on 24 January 1989.

Shortly before his widely-publicized execution, Bundy confessed to 36 murders in seven states; however, many believe that the total number is much higher. Also before his execution, Bundy contacted Dr. James Dobson, psychologist and founder of the Christian evangelical organization Focus on the Family, and agreed to a television interview the day before his execution. In it, Bundy described the influence of pornography on his behavior. While not expressly blaming pornography for his behavior, Bundy did say that pornographic materials shaped and molded his behavior and he would gradually need more violent, graphic, and explicit material to achieve the same "high"; not unlike a drug addict. He claimed that while murdering he was "possessed by 'something ... awful and alien'" and the brutal urge was indescribable. He also claimed that alcohol helped remove the initial boundary for him to commit his first murder. Bundy also admitted that although he believed he deserved the death penalty, he didn't want to die.

Even today, Bundy remains a suspect in a number of open homicide cases and is likely responsible for other victims who will never be identified. In 1987 he confided to Keppel that there were some murders that he would "never talk about" because they were committed too close to home, involved victims who were very young, or were too close to family. Said victims include the aforementioned Ann Marie Burr who Bundy repeatedly denied having murdered; however, Keppel noticed that Burr fits all three of Bundy's "no discussion" categories. In 2011, forensic testing of material from the Burr crime scene did not have enough intact DNA sequences to compare to Bundy's.

Additional potential victims include flight attendants Lisa E. Wick and Lonnie Trumbull, both 20, who were bludgeoned with a piece of wood while asleep in their Seattle home on 23 June 1966 that was very near the Safeway store where Bundy worked at the time, and where the victims regularly shopped. Trumbull did not make it and Wick suffered permanent memory loss.

On 30 May 1969 college friends Susan Davis and Elizabeth Perry, both 19, who were on vacation in Atlantic City, New Jersey—just 60 miles south of Philadelphia—were found stabbed to death in the woods three days later.

On 19 July 1971, 24-year-old elementary school teacher and motel maid Rita Curran was murdered in her basement apartment in Burlington, Vermont. She had been bludgeoned, raped, and strangled. The motel where she worked part-time was adjacent to the Elizabeth Lund Home where Bundy was born and certain similarities to his other crime scenes made Bundy a suspect.

21-year-old Joyce LePage was last seen alive on 22 July 1971 on the Washington State University campus. Nine months later her skeleton was found wrapped in military blankets, carpeting, and rope, at the bottom of a Pullman, Washington, ravine.

On 29 June 1973, 17-year-old Rita Lorraine Jolly disappeared from West Linn, Oregon while 24-year-old Vicki Lynn Hollar disappeared from Eugene, Oregon, on 20 August of that same year. Bundy had confessed to two Oregon homicides but did not identify the victims.

Brenda Joy Baker, 14, was last seen hitchhiking near Puyallup, Washington on 27 May 1974 and her body would be discovered a month later in Millersylvania State Park.

19-year-old Wisconsin native Sandra Jean Weaver who had been living in Tooele, Utah, was last seen on 1 July 1974 in Salt Lake City. Her nude body was found the following day in Grand Junction, Colorado.

20-year-old Carol Valenzuela was last seen hitchhiking near Vancouver, Washington, on 2 August 1974 and her remains were found two months later in a shallow grave south of Olympia; along with the remains of another female who was later identified as 17-year-old Martha Morrison who was last seen in Eugene, Oregon, on 1 September 1974. During this time, Bundy drove from Seattle to Salt Lake City and could have conceivably passed through both towns; however, there is no definitive evidence.

Bundy is also a suspect in Melanie Suzanne Cooley's disappearance on 15 April 1975 after leaving Nederland High School in Nederland, Colorado. Her beaten and strangled corpse was discovered on 2 May by road maintenance workers nearby in Coal Creek Canyon. Whereas gas receipts place Bundy in Golden that day—not far from Nederland—the Jefferson County Sheriff's Office has classified her murder as a cold case.

On 1 July 1975, Shelly Kay Robertson, 24, failed to show up for work in Golden, Colorado, and her nude, decomposed corpse was found in August inside of a mine on Berthoud Pass near Winter Park. While gas station receipts place Bundy in the area, there is no direct evidence as to his complicity.

23-year-old Nancy Perry Baird disappeared from the Farmington, Utah, service station where she worked on 4 July 1975. She officially remains a missing person and Bundy has repeatedly denied involvement.

Finally, 17-year-old Debbie Smith was last seen in February 1976 in Salt Lake City before the DaRonch trial. Her body was found near the airport on 1 April 1976.

Aftermath

During the Kimberly Leach trial, Bundy married Carole Ann Boone. He took advantage of an existing Florida statute in which a marriage declaration in court in front of a judge constituted a legal marriage. Thus, Bundy called Boone as a character witness and married her while she was on the witness stand. After numerous conjugal visits, Boone gave birth to a daughter in October 1982. She returned to Washington in 1986 with her daughter after divorcing him and never returned.

Ann Rule described Bundy as "… a sadistic sociopath who took pleasure from another human's pain and the control he had over his victims, to the point of death, and even after." He once referred to himself as "the most cold-hearted son of a bitch you'll ever meet" and one of his defense attorneys, Polly Nelson, said that Bundy "was the very definition of heartless evil." At one point, Bundy said, "We serial killers are your sons, we are your husbands, we are everywhere. And there will be more of your children dead tomorrow."

Bundy contacted Robert Keppel—the detective who helped put him in prison—while on death row to assist him with the "Green River Killer" investigation at the time. With Bundy's assistance, Keppel was able to understand the inner workings of the mind of a serial killer and was, subsequently, able to identify and apprehend Gary Ridgway in November 2001.

Ted Bundy has been the subject of three television movies and one feature film. The two-part film entitled *The Deliberate Stranger* aired on NBC in 1986, starring Mark Harmon as Bundy. *Ted Bundy* (2002) starred Michael Reilly Burke as Bundy and was directed by Matthew Bright. In 2003 the USA Network aired Ann Rule's *The Stranger Beside Me* that starred Billy Campbell as Bundy and Barbara Hershey as Rule. Finally, the A&E network produced an adaptation of detective Robert Keppel's book *The Riverman* in 2004, starring Cary Elwes as Bundy and Bruce Greenwood as Keppel.

THE TRAILSIDE KILLER

JACK BENSTON

David Carpenter ("Trailside Killer")

David Carpenter, also known as the Trailside Killer, stalked, sexually assaulted, and murdered mostly women on hiking trails near San Francisco, California, with a few victims in Santa Cruz, California. Most of his victims were shot in the head, execution-style, while a couple of them were stabbed to death. Carpenter's reign of terror lasted from 1979 into 1981 when he was subsequently arrested, tried, and convicted of death.

One of his victims, Stephen Haertle, survived being shot multiple times by Carpenter—even though his girlfriend Ellen Hansen was killed—and was able to give police a description of his assailant. Additional witness testimony placed a small red foreign car in the area. Carpenter matched the composite drawn from Haertle's description and he also owned a car that matched the description of the one on the scene at the time of Hansen's and Haertle's attack.

Carpenter was convicted in two separate trials; one in Los Angeles and one in San Diego. Both trials were relocated due to defense attorneys' requests for changes of venue.

He was ultimately sentenced to death and is currently on San Quentin's death row. Carpenter is 85 years of age.

Early Life

David Joseph Carpenter was born on 6 May 1930 in San Francisco—a place that would later become his hunting grounds. As a child, he was physically abused and neglected by his alcoholic father while his near-blind mother was overly domineering. By the time he was seven years old, his stutter was so bad that he couldn't function in any social situation. Many experts assert that his stuttering was likely a result of stress, self-perceived inadequacy, and not feeling safe as a child. Consequently he was ridiculed which made him overly reclusive. Instead of therapy he was forced to take ballet and piano lessons.

To relieve his frustrations, Carpenter suffered from a bedwetting problem and also tortured animals; thus fulfilling two of the three prongs of the classic serial killer triad, with the other being a preoccupation with setting fires.

From a young age he also had an insatiable sex drive and would look for opportunities to express this. At the age of 17 Carpenter was incarcerated for molesting two of his young cousins. He served a year in the custody of the California Youth Authority and apparently learned nothing because after his release he was even more predatory; offending until he got married in 1955.

Carpenter worked a number of jobs, including as a cruise ship's purser, a salesman, and a printer.

Carpenter and his wife had three children and Carpenter's demanding libido got to be too much for her. Eventually his wife was not enough to satisfy him. In addition to his violent rages he would prowl around, looking for other women. When his drive became so desperate, he resorted to violence.

By serial killer standards, Carpenter was a late bloomer. His first serious violent offense occurred in 1960 when he was arrested and incarcerated for attempted murder for attacking a woman with a hammer and knife. He had befriended this woman and invited her over to meet his wife and family. One day he picked her up for work but instead of driving her there he drove to a wooded area near the Presidio and then pretended to be lost. At some point he grabbed her, straddled her, and tied her up with a clothesline. He then threatened her with a knife, forcing her to be still and telling her that he had a "funny quirk" that needed to be satisfied. When she resisted he struck her multiple times with a hammer. Her cries for help alerted a nearby military patrol officer who, essentially, saved her life. When commanded to stop, Carpenter shot at the officer and was met with return gunfire which wounded Carpenter. He was then arrested. The victim survived. The victim described his speech to investigators as slow and deliberate, thus suggesting that when Carpenter feels as though he is in charge of a situation and asserting himself then he loses his stutter.

While initially sentenced to 14 years, Carpenter served just nine before being released in 1969. Tired of his sexual demands and temper—and having just given birth to their third child—his wife divorced him. When questioned about what caused the divorce Carpenter's story would change, thus indicating that he learned to tell people what he thought they wanted to hear.

Carpenter was remarried quickly after his release and in less than a year this marriage failed as he was back to his old tricks. He once tried to rape a woman by hitting her car to force her out of it. As she struggled with him he stabbed her but she managed to get back into her car and get help.

At this point there is little doubt that Carpenter wanted to rape again but not return to prison so he was prepared to eliminate any witnesses.

He was rearrested on 3 February 1970, in Modesto, California, on kidnapping and robbery charges. Before being transferred to prison, however, he and four other inmates escaped from the Calaveras County Jail. After recapture by the Federal Bureau of Investigation, Carpenter was incarcerated for seven years on the kidnapping and robbery charges, with two more for violating parole. He served his time and was then paroled in May 1979, without being listed as a sex offender which he should have been. In August of that year he murdered his first of many victims.

Carpenter found a job at a photo print shop in San Francisco after he left prison and by all measures appeared to be on the right path to becoming a productive and law-abiding citizen.

The Crimes

Edda Kane

44-year-old married bank executive Edda Kane disappeared from Mount Tamalpais Park near San Francisco Bay on 19 August 1979, while hiking in the part of the park nicknamed "the Sleeping Lady" to revel in the glorious view of the Golden Gate Bridge. As she enjoyed an athletic lifestyle and could not find someone to accompany her on her hike that day, she decided to go out alone. When she did not return home that day her husband called the police who sent out a search team with dogs in case she had fallen and required assistance.

Kane's vehicle was in the parking lot where she left it but there were no signs of the missing woman.

She was later found off Rock Spring Trail on 20 August 1979, naked and shot to death. Forensic experts surmised that she had been attacked from behind and then shot execution-style with a bullet in the back of the head based upon the position of her body on its knees with her face in the dirt. $10 was missing from her wallet, along with some credit cards. The attacker took her glasses but left her jewelry.

This was the first murder on Mount Tamalpais.

Kane's autopsy demonstrated that she had been shot once in the back of the head with a .44 caliber gun. As she had not been raped, police were dumbfounded as to the motive for the attack. Nobody who knew the victim could think of anyone who would want to do her any harm and the lack of evidence did not permit police to fully investigate her death. After a short time her murder became an unsolved isolated homicide and things returned to normal until the following spring.

Barbara Schwartz

On 7 March 1980, 23-year-old baker Barbara Schwartz had gone hiking in Mount Tamalpais State Park with her dog and had never returned.

She was found on a narrow unpaved trail, stabbed to death in the chest. A witness who had watched the entire crime ran for help and, thus, led the rangers to the crime scene. The witness was hiking in the area when she saw through the trees a thin, athletic man, about 25 years of age approach Schwartz whose dog was barking. She said the assailant "had a hawk nose and dark hair, and he wore hiking boots." The witness then stated that the man and victim struggled for nearly a minute and then he left as Schwartz fell to the ground which was when she left to seek help. Unfortunately, the witness' description of the assailant was "wildly erroneous in every respect" and she, in fact, later admitted this herself. Consequently, investigators were misled, thus delaying the search for the actual culprit.

Other witnesses said they had seen a lone male in his 40s, wearing glasses, and clad in a raincoat despite the fact that it wasn't raining that day. This man was most likely Schwartz's killer.

The bifocals found near Schwartz's body turned out to be prison-issued so investigators began to look at recently-released convicts, particularly those with a record of sex crimes who bore some resemblance to the witness description of the assailant. The San Francisco office of the FBI assisted with the investigation but to no avail.

Interestingly, however, police in another jurisdiction did question a man who claimed to have been wounded in a convenience store attack; however, these officers did not have access to the Marin County all-points bulletin and, therefore, were unable to make a possible connection that this quiet man may have been responsible for Schwartz's murder. The next day the same wounded man visited an optometrist—Schwartz's doctor, in fact—to get a new pair of glasses. The previous day the police had questioned the doctor about Schwartz's prescription; however, he had no knowledge of the eyeglasses found at the scene of the crime. If he had then he might have recognized the "unique prescription" his new patient had.

During Schwartz's autopsy, the pathologist counted 12 separate stab wounds in her chest, likely made with a ten-inch knife. Several days later, some kids found a blood-crusted boning knife near the crime scene which was determined to have been purchased at a large chain grocery store. A television reporter had subsequently handled the knife, thus obliterating any fingerprints which might have been left by the murderer. Forensic evidence suggested that she, too, had been in a kneeling position when she died.

Anne Alderson

On 15 October 1980, 26-year-old former Peace Corps volunteer Anne Alderson entered the park to go for a jog and to demonstrate that the park was, for the most part, safe. Many witnesses saw her and the park's caretaker even remembered her sitting alone in the 5,000-seat amphitheater to watch the sunset. Earlier that day some of the same witnesses reported seeing a lone male around 50 years of age in the park "just standing around."

She was found the next day with a .38 caliber bullet in her head. This crime scene was different from the others in that Alderson was raped, then permitted to get dressed before being murdered. She was found propped, face up, against a rock with her right earring missing. Investigators believed that "her twisted arrangement" indicated that she may have been forced to kneel as well before being shot.

Mark McDermand—A Red Herring

Police thought they had the person responsible for her death when they investigated a double homicide on 16 October 1980, near Mount Tamalpais in Mill Valley. Mark McDermand, 35, and his brother, Edwin, 40, both lived with their mother, Helen, 75. At approximately 8:30 p.m. deputies responded to a call by a concerned friend. After forcing their way into the home, deputies found the body of a man lying in a hallway who was identified as Edwin. He had been shot in the head and chest. In a locked bedroom deputies found the deceased body of Helen, lying on the bed and covered by a blanket. She had a single bullet hole behind her left ear. Eight spent .22 caliber casings were found near the bodies.

Deputies found a small padlocked door that led to the basement. They discovered a note tacked to the inside of the door addressed to "Shitheels" that said that by the time the note and bodies were discovered it would be "way too late" and that the perpetrator would be found either "on the news or on a 'slab'". The note was signed "Mr. Hate."

Inside the room were spent .38 caliber casings, three .22 caliber bullets, and ankle holsters for a pistol and a knife. This smelly basement room had been Mark McDermand's bedroom and became the prime suspect.

The coroner said that the bodies had been dead for three or four days.

A few days later, the local newspaper and the Marin County Sheriff's Department received letters from an individual claiming responsibility for the double homicide and a handwriting expert stated that the same person who wrote the note at the McDermand's house also wrote these letters. In these letters, the writer stated that he would not be captured alive so on 24 October detectives devised a plan to lure him by running an ad directed at him with a phone number that said that if he surrendered he would be treated fairly.

McDermand called the number that evening and said that he was considering surrendering but that "he had some things to do first." He called again two days later with details about the murders; saying that he tried to kill his mother and brother quickly but miscalculated with Edwin, hence the multiple gunshot wounds. He said that he had to "stop Edwin from hurting others" and that he would turn himself in the next day.

When McDermand approached the police he was wearing a belt with a .38 caliber revolver and also had a set of thumb cuffs and three speed loaders. In his vehicle was a 12-gauge shotgun, a .22 caliber pistol, ammunition, a metal box containing several hypodermic syringes, and some insulin as McDermand was diabetic.

He told police that his brother was schizophrenic and had been deteriorating quickly so he borrowed the guns and then prepared to go on the run after the deed was done. McDermand said that he acted out of diminished capacity and that he, too, was schizophrenic and couldn't remember the murders or when he did he told several different stories.

Nevertheless, the jury found McDermand guilty of two counts of first-degree murder and he received the death penalty.

At the end of it all, investigators resolved his potential part in the trailside murders as none of his firearms matched the bullets found in the victims on Mount Tampalpais. That and the fact that the murders continued.

Shauna May

On 27 November 1980 25-year-old Shauna May disappeared from Point Reyes National Seashore Park while hiking. She was supposed to meet friends the following day to do more hiking. They had selected this area because it was several miles north of San Francisco and had not had the dubious distinction of having had a murder occur there recently. When she failed to show up, her friends alerted park officials.

Two days later her body was found by hikers who had seen her foot protruding from a shallow grave. She had been strangled with picture frame wire, shot three times in the head, and shoved into a shallow trench. She had also been raped.

Her body was found in close proximity to Diane O'Connell.

Diane O'Connell

The body of 22-year-old Diane O'Connell was found the same day and near May's body. She had disappeared a month earlier from the same area while hiking with friends as well and her body was rather decomposed. She had been raped, strangled with wire, and shot once in the head.

It was initially believed that the two women perhaps knew each other and were killed at around the same time as another hiker reported hearing four gunshots in that area of the park during the mid-afternoon.

The two women were laying together, face down. Their collective clothing was piled atop a backpack. A pair of underwear was stuffed into O'Connell's mouth. After investigating, it was determined that the two women did not know each other.

Richard Stowers and Cynthia Moreland

As if finding two bodies wasn't bad enough, police also discovered the bodies of 19-year-old Richard Towers and his girlfriend, 18-year-old Cynthia Moreland on the same day as May's and O'Connell's. The couple had been missing since 11 October, having last been seen by friends who they told that they were going to go hiking in the park. In fact, Stowers was in the Coast Guard and was reported as being AWOL.

Both victims had been murdered execution-style with bullets to the head.

An autopsy placed their time of death mere days before Alderson's, thus suggesting that there were two murderers or that a single killer had gone hunting for victims in two different areas. When ballistics determined that the bullet from Alderson's head matched those in both Stowers and Moreland, authorities knew there was just one single deadly predator.

Visitors were told not to go hiking alone; however, being together did not save Stowers and Moreland. Those who typically frequented the parks stayed away or went elsewhere until the murderer was caught.

Needless to say, the media frenzy that ensued wreaked panic throughout the area.

Was David Carpenter the Elusive Zodiac Killer?

Between December 1968 and July 1969 a man shot two couples on two separate occasions in Vallejo, California and then taunted detectives with phone calls claiming responsibility. One of the victims survived and was able to give police a description. Soon thereafter, editors of three San Francisco newspapers each received part of a strange letter also claiming to be from the killer. His message "consisted of a printed cryptogram composed of symbols and signed with a crossed-circle symbol" and all three of the letters had to be put together to decipher it. A local teacher was able to crack the code which stated that the killer enjoyed killing and it was his intention to continue doing so. He signed his letter "the Zodiac."

On 27 September 1969, while 20-year-old Bryan Hartnell and 22-year-old Cecelia Ann Shepard were picnicking at Lake Berryessa, a man in a black executioner's hood approached them. He stabbed Shepard ten times—five in the front and five in the back—and Hartnell six times in the back. He then called the police to report it.

Two weeks later the killer struck again, killing cab driver Paul Stine. The *San Francisco Chronicle* received a letter soon after accompanied by a torn piece of the shirt Stine was wearing at the time of his death. Investigators developed a number of suspects but none checked out. This serial killer was very clever and turned his escapades into multilayered games before he withdraw and maintained a low profile. This was quite disturbing for investigators who never knew when or where he would resurface.

In 1980, former FBI profiler John Douglas—who had been on the Zodiac case since it began—assisted sex crimes expert Special Agent Roy Hazelwood and San Francisco police to help create a profile of the Trailside Killer.

After examining the crime scene data and photos, Douglas concluded that the killer would be a local man who was shy, reclusive, and may have a speech impediment. Douglas also added that the murderer was likely socially awkward, white, intelligent, blue collar, and had spent time incarcerated. He was presumed to choose his victims out of opportunity rather than hunting the same type of victim. His modus operandi (MO) was to approach from behind and overwhelm his victim—"like a spider waiting for a bug to fly into his web." Douglas added that the killer would also have at least two of three specific background indicators common to many serial killers: bedwetting, fire-starting, and cruelty to animals. Finally, Douglas had said while the suspect likely committed rape in his past he had not killed anyone before his current murderous rampage. When questioned about the very specific speech impediment predictor, Douglas said that the secluded killing areas and method of approach indicated some type of shyness and/or shame and he believed it was due to some physical malady that really bothered the killer. Therefore, he attacked in the way he did to compensate for his handicap. While being very detailed, however, police still didn't have any potential suspects.

After Douglas returned to Quantico the Trailside Killer struck again.

Carpenter was ultimately cleared of any involvement with the Zodiac murders through fingerprint and handwriting analysis.

Ellen Hansen

On 29 March 1981, University of California at Davis undergraduate students Ellen Hansen and her boyfriend Stephen Haertle were ambushed in Henry Cowell State Park near Santa Cruz; another town that experienced a spate of murders during the early 1970s committed by Edmund Kemper, John Linley Frazier, and Herbert Mullin—all of whom were safely incarcerated at that time.

Carpenter approached the couple with a pistol in his hand and threatened the pair, insisting that Hansen permit him to rape her. Of course she refused, telling him off. Carpenter then opened fire, shooting Hansen point blank in the head twice and once in the shoulder. The assailant then shot Haertle and left him for dead. Haertle crawled for help despite wounds that ripped through his neck, a hand, and one eye. He proved instrumental in providing police with a partial description of the murderer: near 50, balding, approximately five-foot-ten to six-feet tall and approximately 170 pounds, with crooked yellow teeth, wearing dark glasses as well as a gold jacket with lettering on the back and a baseball cap. Haertle also remembered that the assailant had spoken in "quick, commanding sentences." This description differed considerably from the description of the Marin County killer; however, the MO was the same.

Other hikers reported that they had seen a man matching the description of the gunman in a red, late model, foreign car, running through the park after the gunshots had been fired.

Investigators were also able to lift some good shoeprint impressions to compare to a suspect when they got one.

Authorities released a composite drawing based upon Haertle's and other witness' descriptions in a number of newspapers to both alert people and hopefully get some leads. Four days later a woman called to describe a man she had met 26 years earlier on a cruise to Japan. She said that the purser on the cruise was a young man named David Carpenter who had been bothering her and her daughter with inappropriate behavior. She also recalled that he stuttered.

Presumably reading the paper and staying abreast with detectives' search for the Trailside Killer, Carpenter decided to grow a beard.

He then decided to kill much closer to home, enabling police to catch him.

Heather Scaggs

On 1 May 1981 police caught a break; however, it would come with another victim. On that day, 20-year-old Heather Scaggs disappeared on her way en route to buy a car with help from a coworker, one David Carpenter; they both worked at Econo Quick Print. She had told her boyfriend, Dan Pingle, that Carpenter "made a special point" of asking her to come alone when she came by to get the car and that his friend was selling it and Carpenter was going to help her purchase it. It was Pingle who informed police that she was missing. Luckily Scaggs had left Carpenter's address and phone number with him.

Scaggs' decomposing body was found on 24 May 1981 in Big Basin Redwood State Park, north of San Francisco. Ballistics from recovered bullets proved that she had been murdered with the same pistol used on Haertle and Hansen. She had also been raped and the DNA from the semen inside of her matched Carpenter.

Anna Menjivas

On 16 June 1981 a jaw bone later identified as belonging to Anna Menjivas was found by rock climbers in Castle Rock State Park. She had been missing since 28 December 1980 and was 17 years old at the time of her disappearance. She had worked part-time at the bank where Carpenter was a client and he often struck up conversation with her. Many believed that he only came into the bank to talk to her. Because the cause of death could not be established and there was scant evidence against him, he was not charged for her murder even though authorities were certain that he had killed her. Her name was added to the list of Carpenter's victims to bring his total to ten murders.

Investigation and Arrest

When police went to Carpenter's house to question him, they couldn't help but notice that Carpenter looked quite like the man in the composite sketch and that he had a shiny red Fiat.

Police discovered that Carpenter had not shown up on any released inmates' records where they initially searched due to a technicality: that he had been released by the state of California to serve a federal sentence and, while out on parole, was technically in federal custody. This issue resulted in the delay and subsequent difficulty in identifying him. That he was a habitual sex offender was another important factor not fully documented in his records.

The police department and FBI set up a surveillance van outside the house at 36 Sussex Street in San Francisco where Carpenter lived with his aging parents and also followed him on his errands, especially when he associated with other known criminals. They approached Carpenter who was walking down the street one day with a shopping bag in his hand to apprehend him. Initially confused, Carpenter then asked for a lawyer; at this point he was told that he was under arrest, to which he, strangely, begged, "Please don't hurt me."

Officers executed a search warrant on Carpenters home and car and found books about local hiking trails and over 60 maps. They talked to Carpenter's former fiancée who told them that he claimed that the gold jacket he once owned was stolen around the time of the Hansen murder; thus circumstantially placing him at the scene where Haertle and Hansen were shot. Further, Carpenter's car matched the one described by the surviving victim and several witnesses, he had the same optometrist as another victim, he had the right distinctive type of clothing, he had a record for violent sex offenses, he suffered from explosive rage and tried to change his appearance with different glasses and facial hair, and he matched many descriptions witnesses gave as the man who had been seen in the area of multiple attacks.

Haertle picked Carpenter's mugshot as the man who shot him and killed his girlfriend. Out of seven more witnesses present at a lineup, six picked him out although not all of them were sure. Police also conducted a car lineup with witnesses identifying Carpenter's Fiat.

He was formally charged with Hansen's murder and Haertle's attempted murder. At his arraignment Carpenter stuttered so badly that he had a difficult time answering the judges questions.

Police were never able to recover the .45 caliber gun that was used in several of his murders; however, a .38 caliber gun that Carpenter had sold to another man, who was on trial for robbery and gladly relinquished it to authorities, was later proven to be the firearm used in the last two murders.

Trial and Conviction

Carpenter's defense attorneys requested a change of venue due to the publicity surrounding his ten murders. However, if attorneys had thought it would make a difference they were mistaken. A change of venue would do nothing to eliminate the incriminating evidence police had against Carpenter. In April 1984, his Los Angeles trial began and on 6 July 1984, Carpenter was convicted of the Santa Cruz murders of Heather Scaggs and Ellen Hansen, and the attempted murder of

Stephen Haertle thanks to the damning evidence that his gun was the one responsible for their deaths. A second jury sentenced Carpenter to die in San Quentin's gas chamber based upon three special circumstances that warranted the death penalty: that he had committed multiple murders; that he had murdered during commission of rape; and that he had lain in wait for his victims. Judge Dion Morrow told the court that, "The defendant's entire life has been a continuous expression of violence and force almost beyond exception. I must conclude with the prosecution that if ever there was a case appropriate for the death penalty, this is it."

Carpenter's second trial began on 5 January 1988 in San Diego. On 10 May 1988, a San Diego jury found Carpenter guilty for five murders. Carpenter was also found guilty of two counts of rape and one count of attempted rape. This trial was different in that Carpenter himself took the stand in his own behalf. He was on the stand for seven days.

Marin County District Attorney Jerry Herman announced that he wouldn't file any charges against Carpenter for Kane's and Schwartz's murders due to inadequate evidence.

In 1994, potential juror misconduct in the second trial was brought to light in that the jury forewoman had known about Carpenter's convictions in Los Angeles for the Santa Cruz murders and had concealed this fact during voir dire for the Marin County trial. Carpenter was not retried as he had already been sentenced to death for other murders. On 6 March 1995 the California Supreme Court refused to give Carpenter a new trial. Justice Armand Arabian said that it was virtually impossible to keep secrets in cases such as this and that he believed that the juror's knowledge had not unduly biased the jury.

In 1997, the California Supreme Court upheld Carpenter's death sentence for the Scaggs and Hansen murders and on 29 November 199 they upheld Carpenter's death penalty from his second trial, with six of the seven justices agreeing that he had a fair trial for the five Marin County murders and had, in fact, been sentenced properly.

In December 2009, San Francisco police reexamined evidence from the 21 October 1979 murder of Mary Frances Bennett. Bennett was 23 years old at the time she was killed. She had been jogging near the Palace of the Legion of Honor in Land's End Park in San Francisco when she was ambushed and stabbed to death. Police reported that she had been stabbed at least 25 times in her chest, neck, and back. Her "butchered" corpse was found under a thin layer of dirt and leaves. In February 2010 San Francisco police confirmed that DNA collected from that murder was sent to the Department of Justice and was subsequently matched to Carpenter.

He remains a suspect in the murders of Edna Kane and Barbara Schwartz.

Aftermath

Some have speculated that Carpenter wasn't technically a serial killer but a serial rapist who killed his victims to eliminate witnesses so as not to return to prison.

Carpenter's case provided the background for Joyce Maynard's 2013 novel, *After Her*.

A series of geocaching caches have been placed throughout Mount Tamalpais in commemoration of Carpenter's victims.

THE TOY BOX KILLER

TERRY CAINE

David Parker Ray was a suspected American serial killer and known torturer and serial rapist of women; suspected because no bodies were ever found. However, he was accused by his accomplices of murdering a number of women and law enforcement officials estimate that he is responsible for as many as 60 deaths in and near Truth or Consequences, New Mexico. Ray purchased and refitted a trailer into what he called his "toy box" which was replete with a number of sex toys and torture items for his victims. He also played a very disturbing audiotape for all of his victims explaining what they will be enduring at his hand. Ray was finally arrested after one of his victims managed to escape after three days of torture. Ray stood trial for kidnapping and sexual torture and was sentenced to 224 years in prison; however, he suffered a fatal heart attack while incarcerated at Lea County Correctional Facility in Hobbs, New Mexico, on 28 May 2002.

Early Life

David Parker Ray was born on 6 November 1939, in Belen, New Mexico. He was named David after his uncle David who was accidentally shot in the heart at the age of 13 by his 15-year-old brother Alden just one year earlier. Ray's grandmother believed him to be a reincarnation of her dead son.

Ray's father, Cecil, was an alcoholic and was very abusive to both Ray and his sister Peggy—who was one year his junior—as well as their mother, Nettie. When Ray was ten years old his father left his mother and moved to Albuquerque. They were divorced soon thereafter. When Nettie decided to stay with her own parents, Ray and Peggy were shipped off to their paternal grandparents, Ethan and Dolly Ray. In the six years Ray and Peggy lived with their grandparents they saw their father twice and their mother only a handful of times. Consequently, there were no maternal bonds between Nettie and her children. In fact, Ray said that he didn't get much affection or attention at all during his childhood.

Ethan was a strict disciplinarian who insisted on the utmost standards of dress and behavior and, as such, the children were required to do ranch chores both before and after school and even though the Rays were not very well off, Ethan made sure his grandchildren were clean and presentable. He was also a devout fundamentalist Christian and made sure to instill within his grandchildren his religious beliefs. Any nonadherence to his rules resulted in physical punishment.

Ray attended Mountainair High School in Mountainair, New Mexico, where he was often bullied for his awkwardness and shyness, especially around girls. Ray commented that he didn't have his first date until he was 18 years old. He was also tormented for being soft-spoken and for having to keep his shirt buttoned all the way to the top—per his grandfather's instructions—when all of the other boys had a few top buttons undone. Ray was also a poor student.

Neighbor Audie Miranda always tried to look out for Ray. He would tell the bullies to leave him alone and stated that even though Ray could defend himself, he remained docile, not liking or believing in violence which was ironic considering what Ray would become. The two became close friends and spent a lot of time together on the Ray ranch riding horses, playing cowboys and Indians, and playing desert hide-and-seek.

Ray always had a love of the outdoors.

Miranda would later say that he believed that Ray's ultra-strict upbringing took a toll on his friend. Miranda even commented that he, himself, was scared of Ethan.

Dolly was not much better. Ray said that he hated her and that she "didn't have a clue."

At the age of 12, Ray began building and setting off bombs and other explosives he fashioned in the woods behind his grandparents' house. He said he blew up a lot of tree stumps as a child.

When Ray was 13 his grandparents gave him a Cushman Pacemaker motor scooter. He discovered within himself a natural aptitude for mechanics and delighted in taking it apart and then reassembling it. The once shy and timid Ray became more confident, especially when his classmates who used to torment him needed his services to fix their scooters.

Some accounts state that Ray began to use and abuse alcohol and drugs while in high school. It was also around this time he began to fantasize about raping, torturing, and murdering women. He said that the few times his father would come visit them, he would bring true detective magazines which Ray enjoyed reading. He began having his fantasies which always involved broken bottles. His sister stumbled upon Ray's sadomasochistic drawings as well as erotic photographs of acts of bondage.

At the age of 15 Ray fashioned his own little dungeon under a large piñon pine tree with a hangman's noose and a collection of broken beer bottles he "planned to use on girls someday." He also admitted to digging a hole and engaging in intercourse with the ground when he was lonesome.

After high school, Ray worked as an auto mechanic.

He married in 1959, joking that he was practically a virgin at that time, and joined the United States Army a year later where he was sent to Korea. The Rays had a son in 1960 and Ray had to return home on emergency leave because his wife was leaving the baby alone when she went out to party. He filed for divorce and sought sole custody. His mother, Opel, and stepfather, Cecil, raised Ray's son until Ray was honorably discharged from the military.

Ray married a second time in 1962 when he was 22 years old and a mere 90 days later he went back to court and filed for divorce again because they just didn't "click".

In 1966, Ray married a third time; to a woman named Glenda Burdine. They were married 15 years and had a daughter named Glenda Jean—who would go by "Jesse"—in 1969. Jesse remembered her father as being gone quite a bit, having worked for the railroad, and of having an unusual fetish for padded leather straps and other bondage fare. She said that kids were naturally curious and while they knew about it, it was not a topic to be discussed.

In sum, Ray married four times, was divorced four times, and had two children.

Ray met Cindy Lea Hendy in 1997 when he was 57; she was 20 years his junior. Originally from Washington, Hendy and her boyfriend John Youngblood moved to Truth or Consequences, New Mexico, on the run from the law for grand theft, forgery, and drug offenses, leaving her three children behind. As she had already served time in jail, she was not keen on returning.

The Crimes

The "Toy Box"

Ray spent over $100,000 on his homemade torture chamber he called his "toy box" that he constructed inside of an old white 15-feet-by-25-feet cargo trailer on his Elephant Butte, New Mexico, property. Elephant Butte is a resort town of approximately 2,000 residents, located along an 18-mile-long, 36,000-acre reservoir.

The trailer was stocked with what he referred to as his "friends": bully whips, pulleys, leather straps, metal clamps, bars which spread the victim's legs, surgical knifes and saws which he used to torture women. Inside this trailer were also numerous sex toys, syringes, detailed diagrams that showed different methods for inflicting pain and torture, and a homemade electrical generator. Ray also mounted a mirror on the ceiling above the gynecologist table upon which he strapped his victims because he wanted them to see everything that was done to them.

He also played a recorded audiotape of himself for his victims whenever they regained consciousness. It began with:

*"Hello there, b*tch. Are you comfortable right now? I doubt it. Wrists and ankles chained. Gagged. Probably blind folded. You are disoriented*

*and scared, too, I would imagine. Perfectly normal, under the circumstances. For a little while, at least, you need to get your sh*t together and listen to this tape. It is very relevant to your situation. I'm going to tell you, in detail, why you have been kidnapped, what's going to happen to you and how long you'll be here. I don't know the details of your capture, because this tape is being created July 23rd, 1993, as a general advisory tape for future female captives. The information I'm going to give you is based on my experience dealing with captives over a period of several years. If, at a future date, there are any major changes in our procedures, the tape will be upgraded. Now, you are obviously here against your will, totally helpless, don't know where you're at, don't know what's gonna happen to you. You're very scared or very pissed off. I'm sure that you've already tried to get your wrists and ankles loose, and know you can't. Now you're just waiting to see what's gonna happen next."*

The rest of the tape involves Ray setting forth his "rules" and "procedures" by telling his victims everything—in graphic detail—that would be done to them to include being raped and sodomized by Ray and his friends, engaging in bestiality, being shocked with electricity, and being poked and prodded with a multitude of surgical instruments and sex toys; essentially, being their sex slave to do with whatever they want. The actual recording is widely available online, quite long, and not for the faint of heart as it is extremely explicit.

In the audiotape Ray describes himself as a "dungeon master" who was affiliated with the Church of Satan and that his slaves were for members of his "congregation."

There was also a videotape showing Ray and his girlfriend Cindy Lea Hendy performing such acts of torture upon a female victim who screamed the entire time.

Psychological torture was also important to Ray. He would blindfold his victims, subject them to brainwashing, use fear tactics, and occasional small favors to keep them "off balance".

Many experts classify Ray as a sexual sadist who finds excitement and pleasure from inflicting pain upon a nonconsensual, submissive and inducing them into altered states of consciousness such as when they pass out from the pain. Such a predilection often forms during adolescence; however, experts do not know exactly what causes one to become a sexual sadist.

Ray had multiple accomplices during this time; including, allegedly, several of his girlfriends, particularly his latest girlfriend, Hendy.

During the investigation Hendy allegedly had told a friend—while she was under the influence of alcohol—that she had willingly participated in Ray's attacks because of the adrenaline rush she got from them. She allegedly confided to this person that "there were four to six people who had been killed, dismembered, and tossed into Elephant Butte Lake." While the friend did not initially believe her, after Ray and Hendy were arrested and the details of the crimes were released, he gave statements to police and the media.

Marie Parker

On 5 July 1997, 22-year-old Marie Parker and her two daughters—ages four and five—were evicted from their apartment for non-payment of rent. They were living in a pup tent on the western shore of Elephant Butte Lake at a campsite called Hot Springs Cove; just north of Ray's trailer. In fact, she had borrowed the tent from him and when her campsite became too messy for the fastidious Ray, he had something to say about it.

Parker was a methamphetamine and cocaine junkie and her main supplier was Ray's daughter Jesse. Ray abducted Parker and took her to his toy box where he raped and tortured her for three days after which he gave Yancy a rope and told him that they "were finished" with her. He then told Yancy to kill her which Yancy admitted to doing. They buried the body in a remote area and Ray threatened Yancy's life if he ever told anyone.

Later, when police took Yancy to the area where Parker's body was allegedly dumped, they could not find any evidence. Yancy stated that Ray probably moved the body.

Police found Parker's abandoned car in the parking lot of the Blue Waters Saloon.

Cynthia Vigil

Cynthia Vigil had been working as a prostitute along Central Avenue (Highway 66) at around 10:00 a.m. when her pimp introduced her to Ray and Hendy in a red recreational vehicle. Ray offered Vigil $20 for oral sex and when she entered the vehicle, Ray produced a police badge and told Vigil that she was under arrest for solicitation. Ray and Hendy handcuffed, gagged, and chained Vigil to a fixture inside of the camper. After a few minutes he pulled the vehicle over and then proceeded to cut off all of her clothing, put a metal dog collar around her neck, place her in shackles, and then slipped a leather mask over her head with no eye openings and a zipper for the mouth. She was also told if she resisted she would be shocked.

When they reached Ray's house, after driving for an hour, Vigil said that she was chained to a bed and was made to listen to Ray's infamous five-minute audiotape before being forced to have sex with both Ray and Hendy. Next, Vigil said that Ray put gravy "up" her and had his German shepherd lick it off. Vigil then had her knees attached to a bar, forcing her legs open and was then "measured" with dildoes that had markings on them before having her breasts and genitals shocked with a portable generator. The entire time Hendy had a gun pointed at her.

The next morning, Vigil was taken at gunpoint to the bathroom to relieve herself and then taken back to the bed, fresh and clean white sheets atop it, where her mouth and eyes were duct taped and she was hog-tied with an elaborate collection of interconnected leather straps. A rope was then attached to a pulley from the ceiling and Vigil's entire body was lifted three feet into the air.

The duct tape was ripped from her eyes and she saw her horrified face staring back at her from a video monitor. She said that Ray tied her legs open and proceeded to whip her with a leather belt, whips, and a cat-o' nine tails. Vigil said that the beating excited Ray who then violated her with a "horrendous looking dildo" and took pictures of her suspended body with the toys inside of her.

Later that day he attached an elaborate system of clamps and pulleys to her breasts and genitalia and proceeded to shock her. Her convulsions caused the pulleys to exert force on the clamps. After taking the excruciating pain for as long as she could, she lost consciousness.

For the next two days Vigil was subjected to sexual torture until she was able to escape.

On 22 March 1999, Cynthia Vigil escaped after being abducted by Ray and enduring a three-day torture ordeal. She was able to escape one morning after Ray had left for work and Hendy had left the keys on a nearby table when the latter went into another room to talk on the phone. Vigil—chained to the wall in the den—managed to use her legs and feet to pull the table toward her and get the keys; however, Hendy noticed her efforts and a fight ensued. Vigil was able to free herself while Hendy beat her and even after being hit in the head with a lamp, Vigil managed to stab Hendy in the back of the neck with an icepick she found on the floor. When Hendy fell to the ground, Vigil escaped the house naked save for an iron slave collar and padlocked chains, and began to run down Bass Road in Elephant Butte. Since she had just been taken three days ago, Vigil had not been taken out to the toy box yet.

Vigil was spotted by a couple of passing motorists who did not know what to make of the woman and didn't stop. Vigil finally surprised a woman at home in her trailer watching television who called the police for her. Vigil was then taken to the Sierra Vista

County Hospital emergency room where the chains were cut off and her battered body was cared for.

When police went to Ray's home, they found bloodied sheets in one bedroom with a broken lamp and broken window, thus corroborating Vigil's claims. A pulley device with hooks and chains was mounted on the ceiling and there was a long, coffin-like box along the side of the bed. Large sex toys were on the dresser.

Arrest and Investigation

After Vigil's escape, Ray and Hendy were arrested off Springfield Road in his red Toyota camper. They claimed that they had kidnapped Vigil in an effort to break her of her heroin addiction. Ray and Hendy were taken to nearby Truth or Consequences—formerly Hot Springs—New Mexico and housed in the Cooper Police Training Center.

Both Ray and Hendy were charged with 12 counts consisting of aggravated kidnapping, conspiracy, and aggravated battery and held on $1 million bail.

Soon after Ray was arrested, New Mexico State Police took the case over from the Truth or Consequences Police Department and Agent Wesley LaCuesta—a five-year veteran of the Criminal Assault and Violent Crimes Division—was called on to assist in the investigation. He left his Las Cruces office and headed north to Truth or Consequences.

LaCuesta interviewed Vigil at the hospital. He observed many small cuts on her extremities, injuries to her breasts, welts on her back, and evidence of her being handcuffed.

By early April 1999, over 100 New Mexico State Police and FBI agents were all over Ray's property looking for human remains.

Eleven days after his arrest, Patty Rust committed suicide after assisting law enforcement personnel with detailed drawings of the toy box over the course of four days. Prosecutor Jim Yontz wondered why the FBI would send a woman into a torture chamber where many women had likely been frightened to death by Ray and the torture he inflicted upon them. He then went to visit the toy box. Inside he found a ghastly collection of sex toys, medical devices, whips, clamps, chains, pulleys, rods, saws, and other items for bondage and sadomasochism; in addition to detailed drawings of how Ray liked to torture his victims, medical books on the female anatomy, and, perhaps most damning, a videotape dating back to 1993 showing a woman being tortured.

There was also a television monitor in the right corner of the toy box so Ray's victims could see what he was doing to them if they looked at the monitor while they were secured to the table. He also had a video camera focused upon the table recording everything he was doing. Photographs of the torture he had inflicted upon prior victims decorated the walls, as well as a bunch of dolls which were "strung up in various states of bondage and torture." In addition to the medical texts, Ray had a copy of Brett Easton Ellis' *American Psycho*; a novel detailing violent assaults inflicted by a man when he needed to release steam from his high-stress life that was also made into a film starring Christian Bale. The novel contains very disturbing descriptions of torture. It was presumed that Ray compared himself to the "protagonist" in the novel as he saw himself as in control and his victims as "expendable pawns in his game", even going so far as to call his victims "packages."

With respect to the videotape depicting the torture of one of Ray's victims, the police were able to find the woman on the tape: Kelly Garrett, who had been married mere days before being abducted by Ray and Hendy. Garrett had been held hostage, raped, and tortured for three days before being drugged and left on the side of the road not far from her in-laws' house. Believing Garrett had been out on a drug binge, she was asked to leave and subsequently moved back to Colorado. Investigators found her in Colorado and she stated that she had amnesia for a long time, only recently—as in the past year—remembering what Ray and Hendy had done to her.

The publicity surrounding the case prompted another victim to come forward with her story. Angelica Montano recounted her ordeal at Ray's hands just one month ago.

Angelica Montano

Montano said that she was a casual acquaintance of both Ray and Hendy and had gone to their house on 17 February 1999, looking to borrow cake mix. She said that Ray left the room and then returned with a knife and told her that she was being kidnapped. When Montano looked over at Hendy, she saw the woman holding a gun, pointed at her. She knew they were serious.

Montano said that the couple grabbed, bound, and stripped her before strapping her to a bed and placing a metal collar on her. She said they then attached electrodes to her breasts and shocked her multiple times in addition to "abus[ing] her with various sexual implements." She then said that Ray forced her to give him oral sex.

After having been chained naked to the bed for three days and being subjected to sexual abuse, it was time for Montano to visit the toy box. Ray removed her handcuffs and led her to the bathroom with a long metal leash attached to the dog collar. He bathed her "like a dog, with a chain and everything" Montano would later say. When she was clean, Hendy applied makeup to her face and then draped a robe over her captive's shoulders before Ray and Hendy led her out into the trailer.

In the smaller trailer—the toy box—Montano was strapped to a gynecologist table where she was subjected to additional electric shocks to her genitalia as well as other instances of sexual assault. She said that she repeatedly begged Ray and Hendy to release her and on the fourth day they relented. She was drugged and taken miles away from Ray's property and dumped on a local highway in the desert where a police officer found her.

Even though Montano did, in fact, report the incident to the police, there had been no follow up. When she saw that Ray and Hendy had been arrested, Montano contacted the police again.

Accomplices

In addition to Hendy, investigators discovered two other accomplices: Ray's daughter Glenda Jean "Jesse" Ray; and Dennis Roy Yancy. Yancy and Hendy had dated in the past.

Yancy admitted to strangling Marie Parker—a former girlfriend—after Ray kidnapped and tortured her. Ray videotaped the murder. Yancy also confessed to seeing photographs of one of Ray's ex-wives in various bondage positions as well as watching Ray torture a woman inside the toy box but that he thought it was consensual. Yancy was subsequently convicted of second-degree murder and conspiracy to commit first-degree murder. He received two 15-year sentences. Jesse was also tried and convicted of kidnapping for sexual torture. She was sentenced to seven years and served three, the rest of the time she was on parole.

Hendy was charged with 25 felonies and was looking at 197 years in prison. To save herself, she agreed to plead no contest and testify against Ray and Yancy in exchange for five felony counts and a 36-year sentence. In the Seventh District Court of New Mexico Hendy pled guilty to two counts of first-degree kidnapping for Vigil and Montano, two counts of sexual penetration (rape) in the second degree for the two women, and one count of conspiracy to commit second-degree kidnapping.

Over 100 FBI agents were sent to search Ray's property but they were unable to identify any human remains. Several bones were located but they proved to be of animal origin. Collecting evidence from Ray's home and toy box proved daunting due to the sheer number of items he had amassed for his tortuous pleasure. In one interview, New Mexico Public Safety Director Darren White told reporters that the evidence inside the toy box was "very disturbing stuff" and "literally made my stomach turn."

It was later discovered that Ray would drug his victims with sodium pentothal and phenobarbital to induce amnesia to prevent them from being able to report what had happened to them when they were released. In Kelly Garrett's case, she was unsure about her own recollections of the torture and accompanying nightmares; that is, until the FBI contacted her and, soon thereafter, she was able to remember—in vivid detail—what Ray did to her so she could testify against him in court.

In his recording, Ray described his whole philosophy about drugging his victims and why getting an accurate body count of those victims he killed is impossible. Ray said:

*"If I killed every b*tch that we kidnapped, there'd be bodies strung all over the country. And besides, I don't like killin' a girl, unless it is absolutely necessary. So I've devised a safe, alternate method of disposal. I had plenty of b*tches to practice on over the years, so I've pretty well got it down pat. And I enjoy doin' it. I get off on mind games. After we get completely through with you, you're gonna be drugged up real heavy, with a combination of Sodium Pentothal and Phenobarbital. They are both hypnotic drugs that will make you extremely susceptible to hypnosis, autohypnosis and hypnotic suggestion. You're gonna be kept drugged a couple of days, while I play with your mind. By the time I get through brainwashing you, you're not gonna remember a fu*kin' thing about this little adventure. You won't remember this place, us, or what has happened to you. There won't be any DNA evidence, because you'll be bathed, and both holes between your legs will be thoroughly flushed out. You'll be dressed, sedated, and turned loose on some country road, bruised, heh, sore all over, but nothing that won't heal up in a week or two. The thought of being brainwashed may not be appealing to you, but we been doin' it a long time and it works. And it's the lesser of two evils. I'm sure that you would prefer that, in lieu of being strangled or having your throat cut."*

One can only imagine the pure horror coursing through his victims' minds as they lay, chained atop his torture table, hearing—in very graphic detail—about what they will be enduring.

Trials and Convictions

The press jumped all over the case and soon discovered that everyone who seemingly knew Ray said that he seemed like a "regular" guy. He did not have any criminal record, nor were there any reports about potentially suspicious activities on his property which he leased from the park service. However, reports from the police indicated that he was considerably worse and darker than he initially seemed.

State District Judge Neil Mertz decided that Ray would undergo three separate trials: for Cynthia Vigil, for Angelica Montano, and for Kelly Garrett. The Vigil trial was set to start on 28 March 2000, in Tierra Amarilla. Judge Mertz suppressed Ray's early interviews with the New Mexico State Police and FBI and also banned the media from the voir dire. Just after jury selection, Ray allegedly suffered a heart attack and was taken to a hospital in Las Cruces. The judge postponed the trial for another week and then there were additional delays and several FBI expert witnesses were excluded.

Then, unexpectedly, Judge Mertz decided to start Garrett's trial for her 1996 kidnapping and torture even though it was the weakest case, evidence-wise. Nevertheless, Judge Mertz scheduled it for the end of May. Of course, Ray was pleased with the delays, not to mention Judge Mertz's exclusion of Ray's printed sheet of procedures for handling his slaves as well as all devices found in the trailer for Garrett's trial since nobody could prove they were there in 1996. This left the prosecution with the videotape and the victim's testimony.

When Vigil's trial was actually conducted, it ended in a mistrial because some jurors were not convinced that the women were completely held against their will and there was a subsequent retrial that resulted in convictions for all 12 counts with which Ray was charged.

Montano's trial was delayed indefinitely because, unfortunately, she was rushed to an Albuquerque hospital on 7 May 2001 with pneumonia where she died an hour later from heart failure. She was only 28 years old. As she was one of only three living, known witnesses who were going to testify against Ray, Montano's death dealt a huge blow to the prosecution. However, prosecutor Jim Yontz was prepared to try Ray for Montano's kidnapping and torture by utilizing videotaped statements she had made at a preliminary hearing on 15 and 16 April 1999.

When prosecutors started "closing in" on his daughter Jesse who assisted with some of Ray's earlier kidnappings, Ray decided to take a plea bargain. He received a sentence of 224 years in prison.

Ray suffered a fatal heart attack while incarcerated at Lea County Correctional Facility in Hobbs, New Mexico, on 28 May 2002.

Aftermath

Yancy was paroled in 2010 after serving 11 years of his sentence; however, his release was delayed because of difficulties stemming from his parole plan which had to be established before release. Three months after he was released in 2011, he was charged with violating his parole and subsequently returned to prison and required to serve his entire sentence until 2021.

Ray is suspected of murdering his one-time business partner, Billy Bowers. The two men bought, restored, and sold cars. On 22 September 1988, Bowers disappeared and his family immediately offered a $5,000 reward for any information leading to his safe return. On 28 September 1989, a fisherman found a male body floating in McCrea Canyon which is along the eastern shore of Elephant Butte Lake. The body was wrapped in a blue tarp and secured to two heavy boat anchors. It had a single bullet hole to the head and $49.47 in a pocket but no identification. There were no missing persons reports for a five-foot-ten-inch male in his late-30's or early-40's so the John Doe remained unidentified for over a decade until Cindy Hendy told police that Ray had murdered Bowers. Hendy admitted that Ray confessed the murder to her and told her that since then he had learned to open the victims' stomachs so they would "stay down" when submerged in water and not float to the surface as was the case with Bowers.

When the body was exhumed and dental records compared, the John Doe was, in fact, Bowers. His son Michael was able to retrieve the body of his long-lost father for a proper burial and some closure.

In November 2002, state police officially opened the toy box to the public in the hopes that renewed media attention might help identify additional victims. Inside were signs that said "Satan's Den" and "Bondage Room." The obstetrical table was still there with all of its clamps, leg stretchers, electric wires, chains, and straps. A steel cabinet held numerous surgical instruments and the coffin-shaped box used to terrorize and contain victims was nearby. Ray's meticulous records detailing what he did to his victims was also available. To ensure that none of his victims escaped, Ray had devised an elaborate alarm system and had written instructions to ensure that all straps were secure prior to leaving the toy box.

However, with Ray dead, the investigation went cold, especially since no bodies were ever found, no possible victims were identified, and no suspicious deaths which might have been loosely linked to Ray were solved. Despite the lack of any dead bodies, he is oft-labeled in numerous sources of literature as a serial killer.

According to Jim Fielder in his 2003 book *Slow Death*, both Vigil and Garrett went on to form relationships and start families of their own.

As recently as 2012, additional evidence has been uncovered which indicated there may be additional victims.

CLASSIFIED AD

RAPIST

VICTORIA MANN

Criminal psychologist and behavioral scientist often find themselves debating on the effects of nature versus nurture when dealing with people who cause harm to others. The argument stems from the possible theories of a person's physiology and biology affects or is affected by the environment in which they are raised. For serial killer and rapist Bobby Joe Long, both nature and nurture shaped who he became later in life. Long was born with medical issues that would plague him later in life. His medical situations would increase as he experienced one after another after another accidents and incidents leaving him with damage to his head and physical facial deformities. These physiological issues would then be compounded by a broken household with an unconventional parenting, a life riddled with early exposure to sexuality, drugs and alcohol, and abuse. As Long passed through the years, his reactions to the world around him and his treatment of people would escalate until he would spend almost two years raping, beating, and murdering a string of women before the law finally stepped in an put in behind bars.

Bobby Joe Long was born on October 14, 1953 in Kenova, West Virginia to Joe and Louella Long. Long was born with Klinefelter Syndrome, meaning he had 47 instead of 46 chromosomes, one extra X chromosome. This medical diagnosis would be an early, but overlooked, warning sign about Long's development both physically and mentally. With the extra X chromosome, males often see delayed puberty, growth of breast tissue, smaller testes, and hormonal imbalances. With a starting point already giving Long problems that would affect him psychologically and medically, the young boy had an unfortunate beginning. Klinefelter Syndrome also causes delayed and slower learning abilities, language development barriers, and usually a more introverted and emotional social reaction to people and the situations around them.

Joe and Louella Long divorced in 1955. Joe stayed in West Virginia while Louella Long took Bobby Joe and moved to Miami, Florida. This would be the beginning of a back and forth living pattern for Long, and where his issues with his mother would start to blossom. Later it was established that Long was often left with the landlord while his mom was out for long amounts of time. It is not clear whether she was always working, or if this is when her reputation for being out with different men had started. Though only two years old, Long would look back as this being when his mother began habits that would later color their relationship.

In the summer of 1957, Long had the first of many accidents that would cause further damage to him physically and result in mental repercussions. That summer Long was pulled under the waves at the beach by the strong undertow. Long nearly drowned and would make the comment later in interviews that his mother was "too busy looking at other men" to be paying attention to him and preventing the incident. A year later, in 1958, Long fell off of a swing while playing. He received the first of many concussions and ended up having a stick puncture his eyelid. His mother took him back to West Virginia and began seeing his father again. Though his mother and father would have an on and off again relationship, they always returned back to Florida in less than a few months or weeks. By fall of 1959, Long was beginning first grade in Miami, though he failed to pass and would repeat first grade the next year. During 1959, Long had another accident. While riding his bike he hit a parked car, throwing him over the vehicle. Several of his teeth were knocked out and Long ended up with another concussion. The following year would be spent going back and forth between Miami, FL and Kenova, West Virginia while his parents tried to re-establish a relationship. He completed first grade in West Virginia.

1961 was a rather rough year for Bobby Joe Long. During the spring he was hit by a car. His face was directly impacted by the front bumper knocking him unconscious and ending with him hospitalized in West Virginia. In the fall, Long ran out into traffic and was hit by an oncoming car. Once again he would have more teeth knocked out, but this time he would be left with a deformed jaw from the accident. At another point during the years of 1960-1961, Long was riding a pony when he fell off. Though he was not hospitalized, the resulting head injury left him dizzy and nauseous for quite some time afterwards. In 1962 Long once again found himself returning to the hospital. This time was from a fall from a fence that caused a laceration on the left side of his head, resulting in stitches. Bobby Joe Long already had the misfortune to be born with a brain altering health issue, having a drowning incident and having six head injuries in less than five years would cause a build-up of scar tissue in his brain that wouldn't be noticed until he had a psychiatric evaluation after his arrest. Ironic, as Long spent the majority of his jobs as an X-Ray technician in varying hospitals.

By 1963, Joe and Louella Long decided to end their marriage again. Louella Long took Bobby Joe and moved back to Florida. This time they would live in a house with several of her family members. So many family members lived in the home that Bobby Joe Long was forced to share a bed with his mother. His home situation in combination with his deformed jaw made fourth grade a difficult time for Long. He was repeatedly bullied and made fun of by his peers. Long's mother began working two jobs, one as a waitress and another as a bartender. When she wasn't working she was usually with a different man. Between her job and social life, she began dressing in revealing and provocative clothing. Long began taking out a lot of his aggression on his mother. He verbally began abusing her, often referring to her clothing and lifestyle as being "slutty." Long felt neglected, as well, due to his mother's absences and time spent with the other men.

Louella Long bought a new home in Hialeah, FL in 1965 for herself and her son to live in. The parade of different men seemed to not only continue, but escalate in Long's opinion. Long began skipping school and becoming more socially withdrawn and more verbally abusive towards his mother. In 1966 Long killed the family dog. His reasoning was that his mother care more for the dog than she cared for him. He once stated that "she fed the dog fillet mignon and I only got hamburger." Long now had a separate room from his mother and began detaching himself from her. He met Cynthia at this time, the girl that became his best friend and confidant. Long also began developing breast tissue, gynecomastia, a side effect of the Klineflter Syndrome, and had to have them surgically removed. Despite developmental setbacks, he had consensual sex for the first time in 1967 with Cynthia.

Bobby Joe Long committed his first crime in 1968. He and one of his friends stole a car. The charges were dropped, though, and Long was never punished for the act. In 1970 he was arrested for the first time for minor theft. Later that year he began working for Arc Electric on a part time basis. Long dropped out of tenth grade twice but would re-enroll the following year. At this point, Long's abuse towards his mother started to become physical. The next year, 1971, he was accused of rape. The charges were dropped and the victim was assumed to be lying would insufficient evidence was found to corroborate her story. Shortly after starting school again, Long was expelled. His view of women was already shaded by his mother and what he experienced in dealing with her lifestyle, and now his feeling towards authority were also colored darkly, causing more disturbing thoughts and feelings for Long to deal with when his mind was already suffering from multiple destabilizing factors.

Long enlisted in the army in 1972 with hopes of becoming an assistant electrician. After finishing basic training, he was stationed at Homestead Air Force Base in Homestead, FL. Despite having the army to help give Long a better direction in life, his inability to stay away from criminal activity persisted. In one day he received seven vehicle related tickets. Though he did have many small setbacks, Long was able to eventually get his GED with the army. Throughout his hardships, his relationship with Cynthia grew. They were married in January of 1974 in the chapel on base. Unfortunately, despite his luck seeming to improve, Long was in a severe motorcycle accident in February. Long ended up spending several months in the hospital suffering from another head injury, damage to his shoulder, and extensive damage to his leg. Doctor's contemplated amputation but concluded the leg would be able to heal enough that it would not be necessary. After enduring one head injury after another since he was a child, Long began to show more obvious signs of brain damage. His sexual libido began to increase, to an extent in which the nurses notating him masturbating over five times a day while still hospitalized. He also began demanding more sex of his wife, Cynthia.

Due to the damage to his body and the possible brain injuries, Bobby Joe Long was medically discharged from the army in August of 1974, after serving less than two years. Long and his wife moved off base into a trailer, where they would raise their newborn baby boy. Since he was recovering from the accident and now unemployed, Long had ample time on his hands. He began using newspaper ads to look for women to satisfy his new sexual appetite. Long did begin to attend Broward Community College in order to try to complete his electrician training he was hoping to accomplish while in the army. Long was once again trying to bring some semblance of balance back into his life, but now the build-up of what he had lost, his inability to handle emotions well, and the behavioral issues brought on by his brain damage, Long began taking out his aggression on his wife. He was arrested for domestic battery against Cynthia.

Despite their growing problems, in 1975 Bobby Joe and Cynthia welcomed a new baby girl into their family. They move to Ft. Lauderdale in an attempt to find work and spend the next several months moving around and looking for jobs, even in West Virginia. Towards the end of 1976, Long's parents help them buy a house in Hollywood, FL. Long returned to community college and was finally able to become a certified electrician in 1977 and even receive his associate's degree as an x-ray technician in 1978. In November of the following year he got a job at Parkway Medical in Miami as an x-ray tech. His success was once again short lived as 1980 rolled around. In June, Cynthia filed for a divorce. She listed the marital issues as abuse and financial instability. Long moved into an apartment in Ft. Lauderdale alone. Shortly after, his bad luck continued as he lost his x-ray technician job. Long then moved in with a friend, Susan Replogle, in order to have someone to split rent with. The stay was short before he moved again, this time with a friend named Ted Gensel. Susan Replogle, then, moved in with the two men.

1981 brought with it, even more problems for Bobby Joe Long. Susan Replogle reported Long for rape. The charges never held, though, due to insufficient evidence, again. Two weeks afterwards, Replogle was beaten and thrown down the stairs by Long. Around this same time, Long began picking up and raping prostitutes. In October, Susan Replogle filed an assault and battery charge against Long. One month later, Long was charged for sending obscene material to a 12 year old girl in Tampa, FL. Phone records and mailing envelopes left Long with no choice but to plead no contest.

Long spent the majority of 1982 traveling and looking for work. During the first half of the year he went to California to get a commercial driving license through a commercial driving school. He then returned and tried to find work as a truck driver. Eventually he ended up back in West Virginia, living with his parents. Both of his parents stated that he spent most of his time there sitting around and not actually looking for work. It wasn't until February of 1983 that he finally got employment as another x-ray tech at Huntington Veterans Administrative Hospital in West Virginia. Though his fellow employees were quoted saying he was "polite" and "a good worker," Long was fired in April for making his female patience undress when it was not medically necessary for them to do so. In June, Long bought a 1979 2-door maroon Dodge Magnum and moved back down to Florida.

In the Tampa area, Long was once again hired as an x-ray tech. This time he worked at Humana Hospital on a temporary basis. In August he met Elise at the hospital. Long began dating Elise, and due to her devout religious nature, even began attending church with her. Long seemed to be trying to put his life back together again and even sent $4000 in back child-support to his ex-wife Cynthia. Long's past, though, caught up with him. In September, Long was giben a guilty verdict on the assault and battery charge against Susan Replogle. Bobby Joe Long was furious at the conviction and wrote several letters to the judge and the charge was changed to neutral pending further evidence. In November, Long was given his sentence to his no contest plea in the exposure of obscenities to the 12 year old girl. He spent two days in jail and was put on probation. In the early part of 1984, Long was officially acquitted of assault against Susan Replogle. Long was still able to continue a relationship with Elise throughout this time.

On March 6th, 1984, Bobby Joe Long committed his first pre-meditated rape through his habit of browsing newspaper ads. Long responded to an ad for a house that was being sold. He arrived at the Port Richie home with materials to tie up the woman who was showing the house. When the tour of the home reached the bedroom, Long pulled a gun and tied her up, raped her, and then stole her jewelry. This would become Long's source of income as he repeated the tactic numerous times and even quite his hospital job to continue his criminal career. His girlfriend, Elise, never questioned where he got the money or the jewelry from.

It was on March 27th, 1984, that Long's new habit would go to the next level and become his first murder. Long picked up Artis Wick in Tampa as she trolled the streets. She was found strangled a while later. Long claimed she had not satisfied him and he got angry and strangled her. In April, Long abducted Mary Hicks and forced her at gunpoint to drive him in her Jaguar. Mary crashed the car, escaped, and went to the police. Long was later charged for damages and only received probation. Though he was getting by on his thefts, Long got a job in May at Gulf Bay Electric in Tampa as an electrician. A new crime spree was formed, though, and Long was no longer satisfied by just raping and stealing from his victims.

May 4th, 1984 was when 20 year old Ngeun Thi Long (no relation to Bobby Joe Long) was offered a ride home by Bobby Joe Long. Ngeun had recently quit her job as a stripper and was walking the streets at the unfortunate time when Long was prowling for his next victim. Long took her to a wooded area. His MO was established during this murder as he made her strip naked, lie face down on the seat, he tied her hands behind her back, and then raped her. Long then took her out of the car and beat her repeatedly before strangling her with left over rope. Her body was found nine days later, face down, naked, hands still tied behind her back, and her legs spread wide. The rope was still around her neck.

Bobby Joe Long was once again fired on May 23rd. Women he worked with and those that came into contact with him stated that he was rude and overtly perverted in his nature. Other employees stated he was obsessed with porn and his work station was plastered with pornographic material. Long would begin a steady of pattern of committing rapes and thefts on women he found in the classified ads on a near daily basis and raping and murdering women he came across on the streets as often as several times a month.

Michelle Simens' body was found on May 27th, 1984. The 22 year old was a cocaine addict and prostitute that Long picked up on Kennedy Boulevard and taken to the local "lover's lane." Long proceeded with Michelle as he did with Ngeun, making her strip down, lie face down on the seat, tied her hands and raped her from behind. Michelle Simens fought back, though, as Long tried to strangle her with a rope. In his frustration and anger, Long pulled a knife and stabbed her numerous times and finished by slitting her throat several more. Her body was found with the rope still around her neck. Her clothing was tossed into the nearby trees. Investigators would get several pieces of evidence from her murder scene, though. Among these were red fibers, human hair, bare footprints, tire tracks, and semen.

June 8, 1984 was when Long found his next victim, 22 year old Elizabeth Loudenback. Her body was found in an orange grove in Brandon, FL. Long had maintained his MO with the abduction and rape of Elizabeth. This time he sodomized her as well. He then forced her to redress and get back in the vehicle. According to Long, she wouldn't stop crying and saying that she was hurting and so he strangled her. She had her debit card and a piece of paper containing her PIN in her wallet. Long used these to make multiple withdraws from her account throughout the night. Her body was discovered on June 24th, badly decomposed and weighing less than 25 pounds. She was fully clothed and still had the rope Long strangled her with around her neck.

Bobby Joe Long spent June 14th with his children in an overnight stay. By the end of the month he was able to get a job at Tampa General Hospital as a x-ray technician. In July he was finally sentenced for his abduction of Mary Hicks. Long was charged $1,500 in damages and three years of probation. Long moved into a new apartment, but once again his luck would not last. In September he was fired from Tampa General Hospital for failing to get the advanced certification he needed to maintain his job as an x-ray technician. He had already built up a bad reputation with female colleagues and patients for his perverted nature. He did meet another woman, Ruth Allende, who he began dating and had a normal sex life with. Unbeknownst to her, Long was a rapist and murder with few signs of changing his habits any time soon.

Chanel Devon Williams was an 18 year old Long picked up on September 30th, 1984. Long proceeded as he had done before in forcing her to undress, placed her face down on the front seat, and raped her. He beat her and attempted to strangle her but Chanel was extremely athletic. Long once again lost his temper, this time he pulled a gun and shot Chanel Williams in the back of the head. Long tossed her body under a fence and threw her clothing out of his window as he drove away, causing it to get caught along the fence and the sign for the ranch he had taken her to. Her body was found on October 7th while Long was raping and killing Kimberly Hopps, another 22 year old. Five days later, Long repeated the pattern with Karen Beth Drinsfield. Her body was found in an orange grove a day later on October 14th. Another woman, Vicky Elliot, also went missing during this time period. Two weeks before Kimberely Hopps body was found, Long was once again spending the night with his ex-wife and children. Shortly after his visit, Long would take another woman, but this time would be very different.

On November 3rd, 1984, Bobby Joe Long kidnapped 17 year old Lisa McVey. Long forced McVey into his car at gunpoint and made her perform oral sex on him as he drove her back to his apartment, something he had not previously done. Once at his home, Long raped McVey, but seemed to quickly regret what he did. According to McVey, Long showered her and referred to her as his girlfriend. He started telling her how pretty she was and trying to say nice things while being delicate with her. Long did try to sodomize McVey, but stopped when she said it hurt too much. Long brushed her hair and clothed her and even made her a sandwich and had her eat. Long's gun was on the nightstand, but he unloaded it stating that he did not want to do anything stupid or to be tempted to use it. Long then blind folded McVey and took her back to his car. He gave her a description of a random black man and told her to say that guy was the one that had taken her. Due to the blindfold being loose, McVey was able to see the car and the landmarks around them while they drove. Long reached a parking lot and helped McVey out of the car, kissed her goodbye and left. McVey ran home and made it there by 4:30am. She woke her father and told him what all had happened. Her father immediately went to the police.

On November 6th, 1984, the skeletal remains of Virginia Johnson were found. The police at first believed that she had been dismembered, but further analysis showed the skeleton had been torn apart by scavenger animals. Four days later, on November 10th, 21 year old Kimberley Swann was driving erratically; she had a history of driving under the influence of drugs and alcohol. Bobby Joe Long coaxed her to pull her car over to the side of the road. Long offered Kimberley a ride and she got into his car. The two ended up arguing, and Long became furious with the woman. He strangled her and pushed her body out of the car onto the side of the road. Her body was found two days later. The body of Vicky Elliot was found on November 16th.

Police got a break on November 15th, 1984. Bobby Joe Long was pulled over when his vehicle matched the one police were looking for. Due to lack of immediate evidence, police took a photograph of Long and his vehicle and released him under surveillance. The next day, the same day

Vicky's body was found, police got a warrant for Long's arrest listing his crimes as abduction, kidnapping, and involuntary sexual battery in the case opened for Lisa McVey. Bobby Joe Long began confessing almost immediately. On November 18th, 1984, Long was charged with eight counts of murder and sexual battery, nine counts of kidnapping, and violating his parole. Three days later Artis Wicks body was found. On November 28th the judge ruled the case needed to be seen in front of the grand jury. On December 5th, 1984, Long was charged with the murder of Virginia Johnson.

Bobby Joe Long was held in prison while the courts sorted through the plethora of murders and rapes to build a case against him. On June 18, 1985, a private investigator gave police a suicide letter, confessing his crimes, that Long had written. Bobby Joe Long was moved into the infirmary for close observation and to protect him from self-harm. A psychiatric evaluation was given to Long in February. The doctor's conclusions were consistent with the brain injuries Long had received over the years, along with mental illnesses that he inherited from his parents and that resulted from the Klinefelter Syndrome. Bobby Joe Long was a sexual sadist with bipolar and manic depressive psychosis. The scar tissue and constant damage to his brain over the years had caused organic personality syndrome and temporal lobe epilepsy that caused him to go into altered states of consciousness. The doctor explained that these lapses were usually what occurred when Long would go into bouts of anger and begin beating, or in some cases stabbing and even killing, women.

The Klinefelter Syndrome already left Long with hormonal issues that caused him to have over reactions and overemotional feelings in different situations. The bipolar disorder was believed to have been inherited from his mother. Long then had the repetitive accidents and occurrences of damage to his head causing constant tears and swelling that then would scar over, building up the tissue and resulting in more problems. With Long's mother having the on and off again relationships with his father, the questionable taste in men, clothing, and work and their relationship souring as it did, Long built a very negative view of women. His anger then became more sexually oriented and resulted in his sprees of rape and murder. Long often felt disgusted by women and degraded them when he could, making them little more than a sexual item to him.

As the year carried on, and despite the psychological evaluation and results, Bobby Joe Long was charged in the various crimes he had committed, from the abductions to the rape and thefts to the rape and murders. Each sentence being more stern than the last. When Long had confessed, he had asked for a lawyer and one had not been given to him. Though he did confess that same day, this would cause issue in the first trial. The first major trial was for eight of the murders and Lisa McVey's kidnapping, abduction, and rape. On September 24, 1985, Long agreed to a plea bargain and plead guilty to all. He received 26 life sentences total and would not have any possibility of parole. He also received seven life sentences that, after the first 25 years, he could attempt to appeal for parole. Though his confession was thrown out, the evidence in the case clearly matched Long's vehicle to the red fibers and witness reports and the semen and prints to Long himself. In 1986, the Michelle Simms trial began in Tampa, Florida. The evidence allowed the district attorney to ask for the death penalty and it was granted. Several more cases began to arise and were subsequentially tried and Long was convicted. Long did appeal the first degree murder and death penalty verdict for Virginia Johnson. The case went forward to an acquittal and became stagnant.

Currently, Bobby Joe Long is on Florida's death row. Despite several attempts at appeals, acquittals of some of the random rape cases because of lack of evidence, the majority of Long's sentencing equates to over several thousand years behind bars and is capped with the death penalty. The fiber analysis came under fire in the nineties when it was discovered that one of the lab technicians was not following protocol. Although Long and his defense team tried to utilize this to his advantage, the plethora of other incriminating evidence along with witness testimony and his confessions made little difference in the effect of the fiber analysis in the case results. It was unfortunate that Bobby Joe Long seemed to be cursed at birth. Being born with an extra x chromosome, his Klinefelter Syndrome caused him psychological issues from his hormonal and emotional imbalances very early in life. Suffering from multiple head injuries and then deforming facial injuries, Long had a very difficult time socially interacting with people. He found himself being pulled back and forth between Florida and West Virginia with his parents' constantly changing marital situation. He then had the difficulty of living with a parent that was gone a lot, saw different men constantly, and living in difficult households, including one in which he would share a bed with his mother as he began the early years of puberty. Long did have chances at redemption. He met Cynthia, the first person he ever confided in, his first love, his first wife, and the mother of his children. He seemed to keep contact with her, long after their divorce, and even tried to stay current with child support and visiting his children. Even though he went on to have several other normal relationships and even good jobs, Long would sabotage each one and always fall back to his habit of using newspaper classifieds to take advantage of women. When rape and theft wasn't enough, Long then began his abduction, rape and murder of women he found on the streets. Bobby Joe Long had a very difficult life and it is hard to say whether he would have led a different life if not for the Klinefelter Syndrome and multiple injuries as a child. Could he have had a normal childhood and became a normal functioning adult? Or was the damage and hormonal issues just an added fuel to the raging fire that burned within him? Psychologists still debate the issues of nature versus nurture and how much that weighs in on criminals like Bobby Joe Long. The only definitive information is that he will never again have the chance to try to be a different person, but he will also never again have the chance to terrorize or end another woman's life.

BLONDE BUTCHER: The True Story of Ruth Judd

ERIN SPENCER

In 1931, Winnie Ruth Judd killed two of her best friends then cut one of them into pieces. She packed their remains inside two storage trunks and boarded a train for Los Angeles with the dead bodies as "luggage".

The media circus surrounding her crime was a parallel of the O.J. Simpson case in the mid-1990s. Reporters and readers alike were hungry for every sordid detail. Ruth, as she was known to her friends, would be tried and sentenced for execution until being declared mentally incompetent. She would later be remanded to the care of the Arizona State mental hospital where she would "escape" over seven times. During her last escape, she would journey to northern California where she would adopt an alias and avoid detect for over six years before her recapture.

CHAPTER ONE – EARLY LIFE

Winnie Judd was born Winnie Ruth McKinnell on January 29th, 1905. Born in Oxford, Indiana, her family soon moved from town to town as her father preached in different Methodist churches.

She suffered from tuberculosis as a child and was sent to an Arizona sanitarium for care. It was there that the seventeen year old would meet a thirty-seven year old physician named William Judd. They two would marry and Ruth would accompany him to Mexico where he was employed as a medic for American silver miners.

William, a World War I veteran, became a morphine addict in trying to cope with his injuries. The addiction soon seeped into his business life and he began having trouble holding down a job. The couple returned to the United States and began moving from city to city. The marriage was not a happy one as Ruth could not produce children and had repeated bouts with tuberculosis while William continued to struggle with his morphine addiction.

By 1930, the couple had a "needle separation", living apart but still remaining on talking terms. Winnie who had usually been called by her middle name, Ruth, had moved to Phoenix, Arizona where she hoped the drier climate would help with her tuberculosis. She had found work as a nanny to children with the Leigh Ford family, who were well-to-do. Upon her arrival in Phoenix, she met John "Happy Jack" Halloran, a successful businessman.

Halloran was married but was known for having open affairs.

John Halloran was nicknamed "Happy Jack" by the press when they got wind of his philandering ways. He was the co-founder of Halloran Bennett Lumber Company. A jowly man with a jovial personality, he used his wealth and status to procure young "party girls" despite the fact that he was married.

The two met while Ruth worked as a nanny for the Leigh Ford family. Jack lived next door with his wife and spotted the frail but pretty Ruth sitting on the Ford's front porch. He engaged the young woman in conversation and found out that her husband was away at a rehab center fighting another bout against his morphine addiction. Ruth confided to Jack that she was lonely and the opportunistic philanderer made his move.

They affair began on Christmas Eve of 1930 up until the night she murdered Anne and Sammy who were also involved with Jack.

Winnie would quit her job with the Ford family and obtain work as a medical secretary at the Grunow Medical Clinic in Phoenix.

It is here where she would befriend Agnes "Anne" Leroi, an x-ray technician and her roommate Hedvig "Sammy" Samuelson.

The two women had moved to Phoenix from Alaska as they wanted a better climate after Sammy had contracted tuberculosis.

The trio would have a tumultuous friendship that hinted of a love triangle between Annie, Ruth and Jack as well as a hints of homosexuality.

CHAPTER TWO – A TRIANGLE OF LUST

Ruth become close with Annie and Sammy, often having sleepovers at their bungalow. The two women soon become friends with Jack who, being the philanderer that he was, quickly indulged in relations with Annie.

This didn't sit well with Ruth who mistakenly believed that Jack loved her.

On October 16th, 1931, neighbors heard screaming coming from the bungalow. But the yelling stopped as quickly as it started and no one reported the fracas.

"I had introduced Jack to a girl they (Annie/Sammy) objected to," Winnie said in a jailhouse interview. "That is what the quarrel was over. He (Halloran) was a friend of my husband but he was trying to kiss my behind my husband's back. And I loved my husband very much."

Ruth had shot both women in a jealous fit with a .25 caliber handgun.

She then dismembered Sammy's body and put her head, torso, and lower legs into a shipping trunk while placing her thighs in a traveling suitcase. Annie's body was not dismembered, instead being stuffed into another shipping trunk.

The morning after, Ruth showed up late for work at the clinic while her co-workers wondered about the whereabouts of Annie. Later at the trial, some workers reported seeing Ruth as having a bandage on her left hand. Some remembered it being on her right. Others didn't remember it at all.

After her shift ended, Ruth called a moving van to retrieve a pair of large trunks and have them placed on a train for Los Angeles two days after the murders.

Ruth boarded the Golden State Limited passenger train at Phoenix's Union Station with both the trunk and suitcase which contained the bodies. She arrived in Los Angeles but her trunks immediately brought suspicion as porters saw the "stained fluid" coming from the trunks which was emitting a foul smell as well.

The porter, a man named Arthur Anderson, confronted Ruth.

"Ma'am," the porter said. "There's something leaking out of your trunk."

"Is there?"

"You know, a lot of folks try to transport contraband into Los Angeles," the train agent continued. "I've seen it all. Had one big game hunter use his wife to transport a dead deer. You wouldn't do something like that would you?"

"God, no."

"Do you have the keys for the trunk?"

"Its in my car."

"Let's open it please."

"My car is just outside," Ruth said, heading out of the depot. "Just wait right here. I'll get my keys, unlock the trunk and then I'll see what's leaking."

Ruth's younger brother Burton arrived in his vehicle to pick her up. Burton, a USC college student, had no idea that Ruth just committed murder.

"Drive," Ruth commanded.

"Where's all your stuff?" Burton asked.

"Just drive, Burton! Don't ask any questions, just go."

The car sped away as Anderson stepped out of the depot. He had the presence of mind to memorize the license plate of the vehicle and immediately reported the incident to the Los Angeles Police Department.

The police arrived, picked the locks on each of the trunks and were shocked to discovered the dead bodies inside.

"I was the chief investigator of the case," retired Phoenix detective Charles Arnold said. "From the police department in Phoenix at the time it happened. At the time it happened, the Phoenix police department knew nothing of Ruth Judd. Never heard of her. Until our police chief, that morning, received a call about nine o'clock, received a call from the captain of homicide from Los Angeles. The chief had said that they had discovered these trunks with nude bodies in them at the depot."

The police traced the car to Ruth's brother but the woman herself had disappeared. Ruth had gone home with Burton then hid in a department store among other places.

CHAPTER THREE – THE TRUNK MURDERS

The horrific crime would send shock waves throughout the country. The press would refer to Winnie as "Tiger Woman", "Blonde Butcher", and finally the case became known simply as the "Trunk Murders."

On Monday, October 19th, 1931, the Phoenix police force entered the home of Agnes and Sammy. Neighbors and reporters were also on the premises, disturbing the crime scene. The next day, the landlord of the bungalow placed an advertisement in two newspapers informing the public that he would be doing tours of the crime scene for ten cents per person.

Because of the ad, hundreds of people came through the bungalow out of morbid curiosity.

With their forensic evidence now contaminated, police nonetheless believed that both Annie and Sammy were shot while asleep in their beds. Both of their mattresses were missing from the bungalow but one was later found in a vacant lot a few miles away with no blood on it. The other mattress remained missing.

Police would also find a letter that Ruth had written to her husband but never mailed. The letter described a multitude of sexual goings-on at the Phoenix bungalow. Ruth would detail straight, bisexual and homosexual trysts that the trio would engage in.

With his wife now a wanted woman, Dr. William Judd put forth a public appeal for his Ruth to turn herself in.

Winnie caught word of her wanted status and would meet with police on October 23rd in a Los Angeles funeral home.

Detective Arnold led the interrogation of Ruthie as they spoke to her in the funeral home.

"Mrs, Judd, don't you think if a doctor amputated these bodies he would have known where to cut them and had to cut four and five places to find the joint?" Arnold asked.

Ruth shifted in her seat. "Well, it wasn't the doctor. I'll tell you who it was. It was Jack Halloran. Jack helped."

"How did you get the mattress out to the vacant lot that the women were laying on when you shot them?"

"I never shot no woman on a mattress!"

"Oh, yea, Ruthie, you shot women on the mattress. Because we found a mattress out on a vacant lot where you set it afire. And it hadn't burned up. And that was where the two women were laying side by each on this mattress. Because the blood spots were in two different spots on the mattress. And now, matter of fact, these women were sound asleep when you shot them weren't they?"

"No, no, they were fighting me."

"Ruthie, they wasn't fighting you. How could they be fighting you when you had them both in the bed there and you shot them straight down through the bed because the gunshots went through the mattress? How do you account for that Ruthie?"

Ruthie sat and stared at the ground. "Well, Jack Halloran helped me do it. And he said I should do that in order to get rid of the bodies."

"I said a while ago you told us that a doctor did that. Now Ruthie your story is all wet," Arnold shifted forward in his seat, narrowing his eyes. "Let me tell you the story. You went out there with this gun to kill these women because this one woman had rejected your love isn't that right? You found them sound asleep and you had the key to the door so you went quietly in there to where they were sleeping and you shot them right through the bed there. Because on this mattress that you drug out to the vacant lot and tried to burn there's two spots of blood not one, not a big spot, not a little spot but two spots in the mattress where the hole went through. Ain't that right, Ruthie?"

Tears began to well in Ruth's eyes. She gulped hard.

"Then you cut them up back there in the bath tub, you want to make this story good about fighting so I said you shot yourself through the hand, didn't you?"

"No, no, no, I never had any gun."

"Oh yes, Ruthie, you had a gun. A little automatic. Same gun you shot the women with. I found the bullet under bathtub that you shot yourself through the hand with."

Ruth broke down and began to cry. "I'm not telling you anything. I'm not saying anything. I'm not talking to you again, ever!"

Upon her arrest, Ruth became the O.J. Simpson of her day. The people of the 1930s were unused to the immorality depicted in Judd's crime-murder, infidelity, lesbianism, and drug use. They was conjecture that Agnes "Anne" and Hedvig "Sammy" Samuelson were "lesbian party girls" who seduced Ruth into their lifestyle of debauchery and perversion along with their mutual boyfriend, Jack Halloran.

CHAPTER FOUR – SELF DEFENSE OR PRE-MEDIATION?

Ruth would describe her murders of Annie and Sammy as incidents of self-defense. She described getting into an altercation with Sammy initially, describing how Sammy took out a gun and threatened to blow her brains out. Ruth said that she fought back and they both struggled with the gun.

"I went into the kitchen to set down some tapioca dessert," Winnie recalled. "We were all in our pajamas. I went to put this down on the sink and Sammy came at me with a gun. She came through the breakfast room door."

"We quarreled violently," Winnie said. "About what I was going to tell about them and what they were going to tell my husband about me and so forth. That I had gone out with Jack. So the fact that it took place in the breakfast room door. I'm naturally left handed. I do many things with my left hand. I grabbed the gun with this hand (her left) and the shot went through there (her palm.)And I grabbed a bread knife on the table and I stabbed her twice in the (left) shoulder. And the knife bent, it was a bread knife, so I grabbed her hand like this (pulling her wrist back) and we both had our hands on the gun and one shot went through one of her fingers. I don't know which one. And one went through her chest. And one bullet jammed and caught me here (her left ring finger), at the top of the gun. And Ann came from behind. She got the ironing board from behind the water heater and came up behind me and hit me which caused us both to fall in the doorway. And we fought back and forth, wrestling for the gun in the door way, both of us on the floor. And the blood was all underneath the linoleum that was the only way it got there it was from the fight. She was not shot in bed like they say! It was in the doorway and the kitchen. It wasn't in the bedroom at all."

Ruth then called Jack to help dispose of the dead bodies.

"Jack cut up Sammy's body," Ruth said initially. "I couldn't do it."

She would later recant on that claim and state that Jack Halloran had called up a "Dr. Brown" and had him come over to cut up the bodies. She said that Halloran had some "dirt" on the doctor which coerced the physician to come over to the home and become complicit in the murder.

"Jack came with me," Ruth said. "And he picked Sammy up and carried her in (to the bed). And he got Doctor Brown. They took me home because I was hysterical."

Ruth would also claim later that she had gone to Anne and Sammy's home for a game of bridge. A fourth woman was there but had left. She testified that there was an argument about Halloran's introduction to another woman and that Annie and Sammy attacked her.

Ruth stated that Halloran came to the bungalow and after seeing the bodies, began plotting a way to "fix things". He went to the garage and came back with a "great, heavy trunk".

"Don't say a word to anyone," he warned her.

Halloran would be blamed for being an accomplice in the crime but after further research the decision not to prosecute him seemed to be the right one, particularly with the half-baked imagination of Ruth.

Her stories would remain inconsistent during her interrogation with Detective Arnold as well.

"So we interviewed her for about an hour," Arnold recalled. "And she'd tell us one story and we'd head her off on that. And then she'd sit there for a few minutes and she'd say well, 'That's right, but I'm gonna tell you the truth now!' And she'd tell us another story. We asked her 'where's the knife that you used to cut these women up with?' 'I never cut no women up!' 'Oh yes, yes you must have because there were in your trunk. Where's the knife?' 'I never had any knife.' 'Well who cut the women up?' 'Well, the doctor cut 'em up.' 'A doctor helped you cut them up?' 'No, a doctor cut them up. He was there. He's my friend.'

It was discovered during the investigation that Jack Halloran and Ruth were having an affair. Halloran himself became under suspicion for the killings and was indicted by a grand jury on December 30th, 1932.

Ruth would become the primary witness through a preliminary hearing which lasted three days.

"I am going to be hanged for something Jack Halloran is responsible for," Winnie said. *"I was convicted of murder, but I shot in self-defense[1]. Jack Halloran removed every bit of evidence. He is responsible for me going through all this. He is guilty of anything I am guilty of."*

Even Dr. Judd, the husband of Ruth, believed that the man with whom is wife cheated with was not capable of the crime.

---

1.   *https://en.wikipedia.org/wiki/Self-defense*

"I know Jack Halloran," Dr. Judd said. "And it is very difficult for me to believe that Jack had anything to do with that."

Halloran did not bother to take the stand during his hearing. His attorney informed the court that Ruth's stories were the rantings of a crazy woman. He argued further that since Winnie claimed that she killed the two women in self-defense there was no crime committed and Halloran was guilty of nothing.

The judge agreed, freeing Halloran in the belief that putting him to trial would be "an idle gesture."

"Jack Halloran had no more to do with the case than I did," Detective Arnold said. "She tried to involve Jack Halloran to get him to finance her defense. And when she fell down on it well, naturally she told a story that Jack helped her cut up the bodies and so on. But she already told that a doctor that helped her but she never would give us the doctor's name."

The controversy surrounding the case did irreparable damage to Halloran's reputation. He would lose valuable business contacts and his social standing in the community. Six years later, he would die at suddenly at the age of fifty-two.

CHAPTER FIVE – A LETTER OF CONFESSION

In 1931, Ruth would write out her "true confession" letter below and deliver it to her attorney. This letter detailed both the events of the night of the murder and her thought processes. Her attorney, Howard Richardson, did not use the letter. He instead had it "buried" as he tried to get her off on an insanity plea.

"I am writing the absolute truth of this case, in full confidence, that you will use it as you see fit in your best judgment. Mr. Richardson, I have full confidence in you and trust you.

This is my first and only confession of the case of the homicide of Anne LeRoi and Hedvig Samuelson. Anne was used to the world, I truly was not. Jack was the only man I had gone with since my marriage. I was ashamed of things I had done. I could not openly compete with her,

I was married and ashamed to. Day after day she lorded it over me, always smiling and fresh and sweet, well knowing she was hurting me with her taunts. Many evenings Anne would kiss Jack and caress him in our presence, then after he was gone gloat over not caring a thing for him but merely working him for money. It was not what Jack did but the continual taunts made by Anne which drove me beside myself . . . I could not stand taunts. I just went crazy. Those taunts kept me awake, I could not sleep. I cried. I even prayed. I wrote my parents to please come to me. I was losing my mind. Wild ideas kept me awake. I took sleeping sedatives, Luminal. I wrote Doctor my nerves were breaking. I couldn't eat. I couldn't sleep. I loved Anne still, but those taunts. I would take more medicine to quiet my nerves, cried to please get things off my mind, to sleep. Friday night I expected Jack. He did not come. I went to bed. Again I could not sleep. I got up, went over to Anne's house. My brain whirling. I was so excited I was panting for breath. Never did I have the slightest dream of hurting Sammy. She simply never entered my mind. Except to get Anne, stop those taunts so I could sleep. Nothing more did I think of. I took the gun and a knife. How I would do it I was not sure. But I had no intention of harming Sammy. Jack was as intimate with Sammy as Anne, but it was Anne's cruel taunts that haunted me. . . . I hid in the house next door. Anne and Sammy returned to the bedroom . . . After they retired, I went to the back door, laid the knife and my shoes outside the door, then crept in the unlocked front door . . . I sat down on the couch in the same dark room and soon fell to sleep clutching the gun. I awakened, Sammy had gone to the bathroom, that insane desire, that power lead me on, I started for Anne. My stomach was turning inside out really twitching, jumping out of me, outside not a tremor, but my stomach jumping like convulsions. I retreated, curled up and went to sleep again. I went back to sleep again. Oh again and again all night I don't know how many times. Sammy kept going to the bathroom, I started for that bedroom and retreated each time so exhausted I immediately went to sleep.

Morning! I heard the milk man. Sammy went to the bathroom again. I started to call her, tell her I was there. I really did. Then I began shaking inside and remembered what I had come to do so this time I crept past the bathroom door, shot Anne. It was a low shot. Sammy called, What fell, Anne? I was hurrying past the door Sammy came out demanded to know what was the matter. I was limp she completely took the gun from my hands. I was non-resistant. I said, Sammy, I am crazy. I have lost my mind give me that gun and I will blow my brains out right here in this door. She held the gun and said, you get out of here right this minute.

... I then picked up the knife and went back after her with the knife. As I grabbed for the gun, I stabbed her in the shoulder, the fight with Sammy in that breakfast room door; her own finger on the trigger when the shot went through her chest; our fight is all about as I have always related she shot me through the hand as I grabbed for the gun; the gun jammed; we fell to the floor, struggled and I finally got the gun and shot her and in my wild state I really do not remember where in the head. I pulled Sammy into the bathroom. I cleaned up the floor I pulled in the trunk from the garage. It was now about 6:30 or 7 a.m. . . . I tugged and pulled and finally got Anne from the bed into the trunk. Now it doesn't sound possible but this all took about two hours. I left for the office . . . I had pulled the trunk with Anne's body into the living room. But the trunk was unlocked. Sammy was on the bathroom floor all day Saturday . . . This all happened in the morning. I stayed in my office . . . until 4 p.m. I then took the bag home with me with the gun, knife, pajamas and dress. I fed my cat and went back to the 2929 N. 2nd Street house at around 6 p.m. I really had nothing definite in my mind. No plans made. In fact except for an irresistible impulse to get Anne I had no other plans. I entered the house through the bathroom window getting a chair from next door to climb in. I pulled the trunk back into the hall tried to lift Sammy into it, but that was utterly impossible, I couldn't possibly lift her, she was too heavy her body was stiff. I then got two cheap knives from the kitchen and severed her

body into portions I could lift. I was hours doing this and then inch by inch pulling the trunk back into the living room."

CHAPTER SIX – THE TRIAL

Three months after the bodies had been discovered, Judd's trial began. Ruth would not be tried for the murder of Sammy, only the murder of Agnes.

Richardson would be steadfast in his defense that Ruth was innocent by reason of insanity. He didn't allow her to take the stand. He kept the existence of Ruth's confessional letter to himself.

The case went to trial with the prosecutors taking aim at Ruth's self-defense alibi. They pointed out the fact that Ruth did not have a bullet wound in her hand when she showed up for work the day after and that her wound was, in fact, self-inflicted to confuse authorities. They further argued that Ruth killed the two women out of a jealous rage as she did not want her husband to find out about her affair with Jack Halloran.

The jurors agreed with the prosecution and found Ruth guilty of two counts of first-degree murder.

She was sentenced to death by hanging.

Ruth then behaved oddly in jail, screaming, yelling and making bizarre gestures. Because of her high-profile case, the Arizona governor gave her a special sanity hearing that took place only three days before her scheduled death-by-hanging.

This hearing became a spectacle for the media. Ruth put on a show, laughing inappropriately, clapping her hands, screaming obscenities at the jury and pulling out clumps of her hair. She then tried to take off her clothes and had to be restrained.

"She's been crazy all her life," Ruth's mother would testify during the hearing. "More or less."

"She comes from a long, lineage of crazy folk," Winnie's father, the Methodist preacher revealed. "Our family has been cursed with madness for over 125 years. It goes all the way back to Scotland."

The testimony worked and Ruth's death sentence was commuted to a life prison term. She was then sent to an Arizona state hospital for the criminally insane.

CHAPTER SEVEN – FUGITIVE ON THE RUN

Ruth would show a dramatic improvement in her mental stability during her stay at the hospital. She no longer displayed the same screaming fits or displays of anger. She fit in with the prison population and embrace the routine, all the while calculating ways to escape.

She left behind a "dummy" in her bed, made up of items around the sanitarium. Fooling the guards, she slipped out of the mental hospital only to be recaptured days later.

The prison guards had her on close watch upon her return but Ruth was determined.

She would escape a total of seven times. On one occasion, Ruth walked all the way from Phoenix to Yuma, Arizona, making her way along the Southern Pacific railroad tracks. These escapes would become a national joke because on slow news days reporters would remark, "maybe Winnie Ruth Judd will escape again."

These escapes would become a running gag among the more sensationalist newspapers. One magazine opened an article on Judd with the words : "When you read this story, the country's cleverest maniac may be at large again, perhaps walking down your street, or sitting next to you."

Ruth would return to her sanitarium after another escape in 1952. Inexplicably, she would be called to testify before a grand jury that was investigating state hospital conditions.

Ever the opportunist, Ruth would plot out another escape during her transport to the hearing. She was searched beforehand, however, and prison guards found a key hidden in her hair and a razor blade concealed beneath her tongue.

A year later, Ruth would have another sanity hearing. During this time she would spent a great deal of time trying to obtain her letter of confession back from her attorney Howard Robinson's widow to get this letter back. She had enough wherewithal to realize that if the letter would be made public it would be incriminating evidence against her insanity defense.

Richardson's widow did not comply but the letter would not be revealed until after Ruth's death.

CHAPTER EIGHT – THE GREAT ESCAPE

Ruth would stage her most successful escape on October 8th, 1963.

She coerced a friend to give her the key to the front door of the hospital and made her way out undetected in the middle of the night.

"About these seven escapes," Arnold said. "The woman, in my opinion, its just my opinion, but I've been around. This woman never escaped out there. She was turned loose every time she went away from that asylum. They wanted to get rid of her! And she wasn't getting seen very fast according to their opinion. And every time she went out of there she'd go out and try to get money from some of her old friends to leave town on and she couldn't get the money. Then somebody would see her and turn her in and then of course the hospital would have to go back and get her. And put her back in the hospital. And that was carried on there for a number of years as I say as everybody knows she's supposedly escaped from there seven times. Before she got enough money to leave town on (laughs)."

Ruth somehow made her way from the Arizona sanitariums to the San Francisco Bay Area where she took on the name of "Marian Lane."

She lived with the wealthy Nichols family, finding work as their live-in maid.

"One of the reasons I came here (to San Francisco) was to be near him (her husband)," Winnie said. "He's buried here in the Golden Gate National Military Cemetery. And when I go down there frequently, I put violets on his grave. I thought he was a wonderful person. He was ill and he was worth saving. And I worked very hard. Ms. Nickles knew I loved violets so she had a whole lot planted so I could pick them anytime and take them to his grave. Because I was buying violets and she said I'll plant the violets, she was that kind and good to me."

Her identity was eventually discovered and she was recaptured after six years of freedom. Ruth would hire attorney Melvin Belli to represent her and he fought her extradition to Arizona. Governor Ronald Reagan, however, personally intervened, sending Ruth back to Arizona.

Ruth would be tried again and judged sane, thus ending her stays at sanitariums. She was sent to jail but only incarcerated for an additional two years.

Ruth would be paroled on December 22nd, 1971. Upon her release she moved to Stockton, California where she lived out the rest of her life without incident. In 1983, the state of Arizona gave her an "absolute discharge" which meant that she was no longer a parolee of the state.

Winnie Ruth Judd would die on October 23rd, 1998 at the age of ninety-three.

THE SCUMBAG

Alexis Malone

Gary Charles Evans was born to Roy Evans and Flora Mae Lee in Troy, New York on October 7th, 1954. He had an older half sister named Robbie who was the product of a previous relationship for his mother. There was also a family friend named Jo Realm who was considered his "older sister."

Gary wore thick glasses in school and was teased. His father also subjected him to regular beatings whenever Gary disobeyed him. He would beat the boy unmercifully with a leather strap, making welts form across his back.

Roy was an Army corps pilot until being discharged. He was aimless after his military service ended, working as a bartender but then becoming permanently disabled after flying head first through a car windshield in an accident. He would then take out his life's frustrations on his family, particularly Gary.

Roy Evans would often make his son stay at the dinner table until he finished his food. There were occasions when he would tie him to the dining room chair and force feed liver to Gary.

Gary would also allege that his father would sexually assault him, "doing vile things" which he "wouldn't wish on anyone."

His parents would have violent arguments and forced Gary to stay in his room, confining him like the future prisoner he would become. He would not be allowed to watch television, draw or do any other pursuits which may have interested him.

His "big sister", Jo Realm, would give him food, passing dinner plates from her room to his because their apartments were so close.

His mother, Flora, worked primarily in retail and in a factory. The factory she worked for closed down, however, so Flora turned to housekeeping to make ends meet.

Flora suffered from mental illness and attempted suicide several times. She would often make these suicide threats in front of both Gary and his sister, traumatizing them. On one occasion, she waved a gun around, threatening to kill herself. When her husband tried to intervene she accidentally shot him in the shoulder.

Flora would have scars on her wrists from slitting them so many times. She would bring men home and make Gary stand watch outside the door while they had sex.

His mother would continue her suicidal ways, one time she threatened to jump off the roof of their apartment building but Robbie tearfully talked her out of it. Sometimes Flora would wander to the railroad tracks and stand in the crossroad, waiting for the train to come run her over.

Robbie would again talk her out of it, convincing her how much she and Gary loved her.

"The whole nature versus nurture argument comes to bear in looking at Gary's background," forensic psychologist Wendy Lipscomb said. "He was abused by his father physically and perhaps sexually. This coupled with the mental abuse by his mother made the wiring in his brain abnormal, without question. He had no one to turn to for guidance really other than his sisters Robbie and big sister Jo. He would remain wired that way for the rest of his life, having more of an ability to relate to women more so than men. His victims would all be men."

Gary's life of crime would start at the age of eight. He had stolen a ring worth over $1,000 in addition to comic books and toys. His mother was a thief herself, shoplifting items at will.

The constant bickering between his parents would end when Gary was fourteen years old as they would finally divorce.

Flora would remarry and divorce four more times over the next three years. She had Gary would move to Potterville, New York but her new husband would prove to be an abusive alcoholic. Later, she would marry a man named "Jim" who was another alcoholic. Going through another divorce, Flora declared herself to be a lesbian and got a girlfriend.

Gary would be forced to live with his older sister (Robbie) and her husband.

His brother-in-law was prone to violence, abusing both Gary and his sister. This would force Gary out onto the streets where he would fend for himself, ping-ponging between the streets and his mother's home.

Gary began to support himself by whatever means he could, mostly by stealing from drug dealers to obtain money. At the age of sixteen, he broke into a home and serve three months for the burglary.

By the mid-1970s, Gary would spend a lot of time being homeless. He would break into cars, trucks, and abandoned buildings. Eventually, he would live with two childhood friends. One was a man named Michael Falco who reportedly tortured and sexually abused animals. The other was fellow thief, Timothy Rysedorph. Gary would live in a shed behind their apartment before he moved in.

"They played baseball or stick ball or something when they were little kids," Dana Rysedorph, the wife of Tim said. "They rode their bikes together and did the things that little kids do. And they may have shared an apartment when (Rysedorph) was about 19."

"But since I started dating Tim, I never saw the man (Gary Evans)," Dana said. "The first time I saw the man was when the police showed me a mug shot. I'd like to know when Tim had time to fit this in. All he ever did was work and spend time with us. But because he knew (Evans, he's supposed to be side-by-side with him?"

Having these two partners in crime, Gary would step up his thievery, becoming adept at appraising antiques and jewelry. He would run a con on local antique dealers, pretending to be an expert. He would study their storefronts for openings in which he could later break in.

Both Falco and Rysedorph would assist him in these antique store burglaries. The trio would bypass store alarms by tunneling outside the walls in order to enter the store undetected.

Evans would be convicted for fifteen antique-store robberies over the course of his life.

"Gary was the ringleader of the group of friends from around his block," Lipscomb said. "He held no emotions for them, however. He viewed them as a means to an end, people that he could use and later discard if they proved to be a liability. For the most part, he was a loner. He could sleep out in the woods and go for long periods of time without the need for any contact. He didn't so much have friendships with men as much as he had partners in crime."

Gary would have many girlfriends, mainly Deirdre Fuller. The two would date from 1977 until 1990 but the relationship would be a tumultuous one. He was okay with her dating other men, as long as they were Caucasian. When Deirdre began dating a black man, Gary became enraged.

He wanted everything he had ever given her back.

"I would like to kill a woman and a nigger," he would later state to friends.

On January 13th, 1977, Gary would be caught burglarizing a home in Lake Place, New York. He would be sentenced to four years in prison, being held at the Clinton Correctional Facility in Dannemora, New York.

Six months later, his father would die of throat cancer while Gary was held in jail.

He would serve two years of the four year sentence until his release. When he got out, he went back into the same pattern of petty theft with Tim Rysedorph and Michael Falco.

They would use their apartment as a fencing headquarters for all of their stolen goods before renting out a storage unit.

The trio would evade capture for almost a year until Gary was stopped by police and caught with a few hundred dollars in stolen goods.

Gary, still on parole, was immediately sent back to prison, this time to the old Rensselaer County Jail in downtown Troy, New York.

On this occasion, however, he would befriend some Hells Angels inside who engineered an escape. Gary would be captured five hours after fleeing the prison and be punished with solitary confinement.

Gary would remain in prison and be denied parole this time around.

The New York State Department of Corrections then transferred him to Attica State Prison which housed the most violent criminals. Gary was spared being placed in the general population but it is here that Jim Horton, the chief investigator of his crimes, believed that Gary turned violent.

He would work as an informant for Jim Horton, telling them of impending petty crimes that he knew were about to take place, setting up a large drug bust with a man named Archie Bennett.

"Gary was a good talker when he wanted to be," Lipscomb said. "He knew he could charm and he couldn't. By running cons in the antique business, he quickly learned the art of negotiation. He was able to parlay this skill in getting a 'job' of sorts as an informant."

Gary would be released from prison on December 29th, 1982 but once again return to his old pals, particularly Michael Falco.

Two months later, however, Gary's mother would die in a freak accident. She fell on some ice while entering her car and hit her head on the bumper.

Gary grieved but soon returned to his life of crime with Falco and Rysedorph. He would break into a home on Easter, 1983 and once again be arrested.

Back in prison, he remained there for a year before being set free on a "conditional release program." This mandated that he had to be on his best behavior for the remaining nine months of his sentence.

Gary would scoff at the court order. He went back to burglarizing homes as soon as he was released. Teaming up with Falco, the two thieves would not get caught over the next nine months.

On February 16th, 1985, the duo would go to East Greenbush, New York in Falco's brown Plymouth. They had two large duffel bags, a police scanner, a rope ladder and other burglary tools.

Parking behind an antique shop, they propped up a portable toilet and made their way to the top of the roof.

Gary and Falco then dropped down from a hatch on the roof. In just minutes, they would fill the duffel bags with whatever they could; gold, jewelry, valuables all tallying up to $15,000.

They climbed back out of the store and whooped and hollered at the size of their stolen booty.

A cop, however, pulled up behind them as they were about to leave.

He asked what they were doing behind the building and the two men casually explained that they had to "take a piss."

The cop took their identification down and let the two thieves go, Gary's charm enabling them to get away.

"At this point of his life, Gary was a career criminal," Lipscomb said. "He was intelligent, with the ability to meticulously plan a robbery. He could walk into a store and see the ways in and out, ways in which the ordinary person would never dream. But for all this intelligence he could not see the trajectory that his life was on. He was only intelligent in certain things. He did not have a clue when it came to living a sustainable life. He was one a road destined to prison and true to like minded criminals he did nothing to get off that path. He embraced it instead."

On April 21st, 1985, Gary went to Troy, New York to sell dope to two marijuana dealers. The dealers gave him the money ($12,000) and when they went to his trunk to retrieve the marijuana, Gary sprinted away. The two men gave chase and Gary circled back around, getting into their vehicle and speeding away.

The dope dealers then called the police, telling them that Gary had robbed them of both the money and the car by gunpoint.

Making his way into Cohoes, New York, Gary would run a red light.

A cop immediately pulled him over but Gary thought the officer was stopping him for the robbery. Gary then threw his gun and fake identification out of the vehicle before sprinting out of the car. The cops eventually found him and sent him to the Albany County Jail.

On July 1985, he was sentenced to another two to four years before being moved to the Renssaler County Jail.

Upon his release, Gary would commit his first murder in shooting his burglary partner, Michael Falco. Rysedorph had told Gary that Falco had stolen some jewelry from him. Rysedorph said that Falco had given the jewelry to a female friend. This enraged Gary and he decided to kill his childhood friend.

Gary would use a .22 caliber pistol with a homemade silencer (he would make the silencer himself with parts of a screen door and duct tape)

He enlisted the aid of Rysedorph to put Falco's body in the trunk of his own car, wrapping the corpse up in a sleeping bag.

The two then drove to Lake Worth, Florida to visit Gary's sister Robbie.

They would bury the body near her house and would stay in Florida. It would later be revealed that Rysedorph had lied and the truth was that he had stolen the jewelry.

"Gary had now made the progression from small-time thief to drug dealer and murderer," Lipscomb said. "This does fit the psychological profile given his background. He endured parental abuse and would torture animals (he once tied up the tail of a cat and set it on fire.)

Bouncing in and out of jail had no doubt lowered his inhibitions. Whatever remorse or hesitation he felt was now out the window. He would commit whatever crime he felt would be necessary and his mindset would be the same. 'Don't get caught, don't get caught.' If anyone around him was careless or looked like they would prospectively betray him, they would be killed. Falco was the first of many."

Gary would then return to prison after being caught for another burglary. His sister Robbie would write Gary in prison. She wouldn't visit and hardly ever wrote so Gary was scratching his head upon receiving her letter. Robbie would write that someone was calling her, disguising their voice as Gary's. This person would say that he was into bestiality and bragged about having sex with farm animals.

It was yet another episode in an increasing series of bizarre occurrences in Gary's life. While in prison, he began fantasizing about an ex-girlfriend, Stacy, someone he had not seen in over fifteen years. Gary wanted to find her and then kill anyone who got in his way who tried to stop him. Gary would never admit to being homosexual but it was reported that he had relationships with transsexuals in prison. Later, he would have a friend come over and discover his collection of homosexual magazines, dildos and other gay sex toys.

In December of 1986, Gary would be moved to the Clinton Correctional Facility. He was placed under protective custody as he convinced authorities that the Hells Angels were out to kill him.

Gary would complain that he was being held until March of 1988 when his release date should have been in December of 1987. He then wrote a letter to Torri Ellis (Falco's common-law wife) and inquired if she heard anything about Falco, knowing full well that he killed the man.

While in prison, Gary would befriend David "The Son Of Sam" Berkowitz who was a serial killer of young girls. David would call Gary "The Great Tricep King" in reference to his muscular arms. The serial killer would anger Gary, however, when he gave him a muscle magazine which featured a black bodybuilder. David would later apologize to Gary as he didn't realize how racist his fellow mate was.

The two would lift weights together but during one session Gary would call his new friend "David Berserk-o-witz" which would end up in a shouting match between the two.

His troubles in jail didn't end with the Son of Sam. Beefed up with the weight training, Gary entered a child molester's cell and "body slammed him all over."

He was then sent to solitary confinement for two weeks before being once again released in March of 1988.

"During this last foray in prison, Gary would come out even more sociopathic than before," Lipscomb said. "He now had a new physique, building up his arms and back. He would use this to intimidate drug dealers in the area and his future partners in crime. It was a classic case of 'show me your friends and I'll show you your future.' He had spent the majority of his adult life amongst criminals in jail. Now, armed with a new physique, he would be ready to take his game to another level."

Gary would befriend a new partner in crime, Damien Cuomo, and the duo would pride themselves on being intelligent thieves. The pair would be smarter and more prolific than before, even going so far as wearing shoes that were three and four sizes too big to throw off the investigators.

As part of his parole, however, Gary had to get a job. He always thought jobs were for suckers and that they were "too hard."

Investigator Horton seemed to take pity on him, however, and set the lifetime thief up for different jobs. Gary would work at a cemetery digging holes but couldn't make it past the first five days. Ironically, while he was in prison, he was forced to work. Gary was an amateur artist and the prison authorities made him make greeting cards. This earned him $7 a week which he used to buy junk food with Twinkies being his favorite.

After the cemetery job fell through, Gary got a job at a garden nursery where he would do all of the heavy lifting. He worked sporadically, more comfortable with commiting burglaries on the side.

Gary would stay out of trouble for almost a year until March of 1989. He and Cuomo were on their way to a job when a cop pulled them over. The officer searched their trunk and found ski masks, stun guns, a police scanner, walkie-talkies, crowbars, screwdrivers, duct tape, ropes, handcuffs, gloves, hats, maps, and a book on police radio frequencies.

The cop did not discover that the duo had hidden stolen goods in the door panels and under a carpet in the trunk.

He did have enough to book the lifelong criminals, however.

"Gary was a hopeless case at this point," Lipscomb said. "He was advancing in age and could never adjust to a normal nine-to-five. He had disdain for an honest days work and preferred the quick hit of a burglary. At this point, he is also a travesty of the criminal justice system. He had been in and out of jail over twenty-three times, they still can't pin the Falco murder on him, yet they keep letting him out of jail."

After a brief jail term, Gary would be released and immediately pick up where he left off with Cuomo.

On September 8th of 1989, they would kill Douglas Berry, a store owner asleep in his shop after hours.

Gary and Cuomo did not realize that Berry was still in the store when they had broken in. Berry was asleep but the breaking glass awoke him. He discovered the two men in his store but Gary would shoot him once in the head with his .22 caliber gun.

The shot would be fatal.

The duo ran out of the store, leaving Berry's body in full view.

Gary would monitor the news with anxiety until police arrested another man for the murder. This innocent man was soon released, however, and the police remained in the dark in who shot Douglas Berry.

Three months later, Gary would kill his partner, Damien Cuomo. He believed that he should have gotten more money for their robbery as he only got $15,000. He shot him three times in the back of the head after handcuffing Cuomo's hands behind his back. He wrapped up Cuomo's body with a shower curtain, blanket and tied it all together with a rope.

Gary had dug a hole at his place weeks before and hid Cuomo's body inside, covering it with a makeshift door and dirt.

He then went on the run to Florida with his girlfriend, bringing her along so it looked as if he was not hiding something.

In the summer of 1990, he still had Stacy (his teenage girlfriend/fantasy) on his mind. It had been over fifteen years since he had seen her and he daydreamed about taking her away from her husband

Gary followed up on his warped fantasy. He showed up at her workplace but Stacy made it clear that she did not want anything to do with him. He then went back to New York and in October of 1981, he would kill another jewelry shop owner named Gregory Jouben.

This killing would be pre-planned.

Gary entered the store and pretended that he was looking to by some jewelry. He waited until Jouben looked down to retrieve a piece when Gary shot him three times in the back of the head with his .22 caliber pistol.

Gary had placed a pillow case around his gun to catch the shells. He would then steal over $60,000 worth of valuables from Jouben.

In a panic, the now confirmed serial killer would flee to Colorado but then return. He placed the gun that he killed Jouben with into a metal box and buried it in the back of Albany Rural Cemetery.

Always the opportunist, Gary would steal a marble bench from the cemetery (it weighed one thousand pounds) and bring it back to New York, successfully selling it days later. He would also steal a 300-pound brass eagle which stood atop an obelisk marking Col. Ernest Ellsworth's grave.

"With the killing of Cuomo," Lipscomb said. "Gary no longer had a regular partner. So he had to strong arm some of his burglaries as was the case with the Jouben murder. He wouldn't be able to break in by himself so instead he takes a more direct approach. This new bold attitude bespeaks of his growing arrogance. Even if he goes to jail he will come right back out. He's a man that will steal anything that isn't nailed down. Even if it is nailed down, he'll try and take out the nails."

In March of 1993, Gary would break into the bathroom window of the antique shop of Kathy Alexander. He would steal diamonds, gold, a rare handbag valuing up to $20,000.

For whatever reason, Gary had a fetish for hanging out in cemeteries. He would try to steal another marble bench from a cemetery but this time graveyard security spotted him. Once again, he would be throw in jail but only for a month.

Seeking new opportunities, he would break into the Norman Williams Public Library in Woodstock, Vermont and steal the Birds of America book by James Audubon. This was bad news for Gary as not only was the book priceless but a federal judge was on the Board of Trustees for the library. He would give himself up for stealing the book and be sentenced to 27 months in jail. Gary would serve only thirteen months and upon his release, he would kill his former partner Timothy Rysedorph.

Rysedorph was helping Gary clean out their storage facility where they kept their stolen goods. Gary then turned the gun on Rysedorph, killing him.

Rysedorph would reported missing by his wife, Dana.

He had called her earlier from a Dunkin Donuts restaurant and said he would be home within the hour. His car would be found the next day.

Rysedorph would leave a note on the table for his family which said "Have a good day. See you later. I love you."

Dana and his then nine year old son Timmy would hope for the best to no avail.

Gary had cut up Rysedorph's body with a chainsaw, sectioning the limbs off in five pieces. He bagged each body part then placed them into cardboard boxes. He then drove to a hill in Brunswick, New York where he buried the boxes in a shallow grave. He tossed the gun and chain saw into the Hudson river.

Gary would cover his tracks, deciding to call Lisa (Cuomo's girlfriend) and inquire about Tim Rysedorph.

"Lisa? Lisa Morris?"

"Yeah?"

"This is Lou," he said in an angry voice. "Where's Tim (Rysedorph)?"

"Who's this?"

"This Lou."

"I don't know. Who are you?"

"I'm a friend of his from work. I'm returning his call."

"I haven't heard from him."

"Hmmm," Gary said. "He might be in some trouble, girl. He might be in some trouble."

Still on probation, Gary disappeared for seven months. He would call Lisa again, telling her that what happened to Mike (Falco) probably happened to Tim (Rysedorph) but that Cuomo was probably living it up in the Carolinas. He would befriend the woman, giving her all kinds of stories of why Cuomo was not coming back. He needed a place to stay and she allowed him to live there.

Police would finally trace the killing of Rysedorph back to him. He would be captured in Jonesbury, Vermont.

Gary would confess to the five killings and then be transferred to Albany County jail where he would remain in protective lock down.

He would then lead detectives to where he buried the bodies of Tim Rysedorph and Damien Cuomo.

Investigator Jim Horton then made Gary call Lisa Morris again and tell her that he had killed Cuomo after having her believe for so long that he was still alive.

The woman was flabbergasted. She could not believe that Gary had lied to her and for so long.

Gary was transferred to the Rensselaer County Jail in downtown Troy but nixed the idea when they realized that that part of the jail was under reconstruction. He was considered a serious flight risk and admitted to both investigator Horton and Jo Rehm that he will try to escape.

The district attorney decided to try him as a capital offender and have him executed by lethal injection.

Gary would have his hearing at the Albany Jail in Colonie, New York. During his transport, he kicked out the window of the police van while the vehicle was traveling across the Troy-Menands bridge over the Hudson river.

"They were traveling about 60 miles an hour when he apparently threw both his feet through the window and shattered it," Troy Fire Chief Robert Essigan said. "Somehow he jumped out the window, over the guardrail and into the water."

Evans had his hands shackled behind him and his feet chained together as he was riding in the rear of the caged U.S. Marshals van.

The trip was only supposed to last twenty minutes. A second vehicle with two additional deputy U.S. Marshalls followed as Evans made his way back to the Rensselaer County Jail.

He then dove onto the roadway through the side window. The vehicles screeched to a halt.

Deputies then chased Evans who had "hobbled" over to the side of the road before jumping off the bridge.

Witnesses would call the police as they initially thought Evans was a construction worker with his orange coveralls.

Gary had taken off his handcuffs and flipped off the US Marshalls as he fell to his death.

"There was really nothing they could do," Essigan said. "This guy was quite an escape artist. He was good, and I guess this was his spectacular ending."

He left behind a suicide letter expressing regret that he would not be able to spend time with Doris Sheehan, the woman he loved.

His final words were sent to lawyer Randolph Treece, whom he addressed in a letter. "No lessons here are learned, onto a better place now," Evans wrote. "My friends are happy and I'm already there with Canis Minor (a star of the constellation Orion) and a Beautiful Blue Moon with a smile, stars surround me and peace and love are mine. They can't be taken or touched."

"I win," were the last words he wrote, underlining "win."

His body would be recovered and during the autopsy the medical examiner would find a razor blade and a paper clip taped to his ankle under his sock.

Gary also had a handcuff key stuffed up his left nasal passage with another razor blade shoved very deep inside his nose.

Relatives of his victims felt no remorse when they learned of Gary's suicide.

"It couldn't have happened to a nicer guy," Mary Deeb said, the sister of Michael Falco. "I'll probably go to hell for that but I can't help it. That's the way I felt. It's terrible to feel so relieved that someone jumped to his death but I cant help it."

"I'm going to tell you, when I saw him on TV and he had this very smug, arrogant, non-remorseful look on his face. I knew he's no good," Sal Falco said, the older brother of Michael. "I think there's a higher power that says it's time for you to stand in my court and there's a tougher jury up there."

"Forgive? Forgive him for killing my brother? No way. There's no reason to kill my brother. He didn't do anything wrong. He didn't deserve that kind of a sentence."

"He killed Michael when he was 26," Elaine DiMauro said, Falco's former girlfriend and mother of his two children. "He had a family and two children to look forward to. I was hoping he would go to jail. Justice still hasn't been served."

"I think the gates of hell are opening wide open for this man. The fires are burning pretty crisp. I hope to God they suffocate him."

SMELLY BOB
OSCAR VALDEZ

Robert Black (Smelly Bob)

Robert Black, also known as "Smelly Bob" was a Scottish pedophile and serial killer who preyed on young girls in the United Kingdom. Between 1981 and 1986, Black was convicted of the kidnap, sexual assault, and murder of four girls—plus the kidnapping and rape of another young girl and the attempted kidnapping of yet another—between the ages of five and 11 and was sentenced to life in prison with a minimum of 35 years. Black is also suspected of being responsible for the murders of 12 other girls between 1969 and 1987 in England, Ireland, and continental Europe. Black died of natural causes on 12 January 2016 while incarcerated at HMP Maghaberry, just weeks before he was to be charged with the murder of another of his victims.

Early Life

Robert Black was born on 21 April 1947 in Grangemouth, Stirlingshire, Scotland, the illegitimate son of Jessie Hunter Black who was 24 at the time and an unknown father whose name was never put on Black's birth certificate. Jessie earned a pittance as a factory worker and was in no position to care for a child, let alone an illegitimate one which carried with it a large social stigma. So, when he was six months old Black's mother had him fostered. He was subsequently raised by experienced, middle-aged couple Jack and Isabel Tulip who lived in Kinlochleven. Black initially adopted their surname and lived with them until 1958 when his foster mother died; his foster father having already passed away when Black was five. When Margaret died, Black was only 11 years of age.

In the meantime Black's mother married Francis Hall, had four more children who never even knew that they had a half-brother, and moved to Australia. She died in 1982 without ever having any contact with the son she gave away.

Locals remember how young Black was usually heavily-bruised as a child; however, Black himself does not remember how he sustained most of the injuries. He did recall how Margaret used to lock him in the house as punishment for poor behavior or would spank his bare bottom with a belt. During the night, Black feared that there was a monster under his bed and he suffered from a recurring nightmare that featured a "big hairy monster" in a cellar full of water. When he awakened, he found that he had typically wet the bed, for which he was invariably beaten.

In school he was referred to as "Smelly Robbie Tulip" and is remembered to this day as "aggressive and slightly wayward" as well as being a loner with a tendency to bully. Black preferred the company of younger children who he could easily dominate. Instead of joining a "gang" of classmates his age, he started his own and all of the members were several years younger than he. Compounding the problem was that Black demonstrated "sudden, mindless violence perpetrated against those physically less able than himself."

The local bobbie, Sandy Williams, remembers Black as a "wild wee laddie" who "didn't give a damn" or have respect for authority and that he had a "dangerous spirit" and "needed a smack round the ear to keep him in line." However, the entire time Black lived with the Tulips he was never in serious trouble; just childish fights, bullying younger children, swearing, and other normal trouble at school—nothing that merited more than a rebuke from Williams.

When Margaret died when Black was 11 years of age, it was one of the worst possible things imaginable because now he was, again, deprived of a mother. Black was subsequently placed with another foster family in Kinlochleven. He only lived with them a short time because not long after his placement he dragged a young girl into a public bathroom and sexually fondled her. His new foster mother reported the offense to social workers and insisted that Black be placed elsewhere. Black was then sent to the Redding Children's home, a mixed-gender children's home near Falkirk, close to where he was born.

From a young age Black exhibited significant antisocial tendencies, particularly a disturbing awareness of and fascination with sex and women's vaginas. At the age of five he and a girl compared their genitalia. At the age of seven at a school dance he preferred lying on the floor and staring up girls' dresses instead of actually dancing. At the age of eight he took off a neighbor's baby's diaper while he was babysitting to look at her vagina. Despite being heterosexual, Black stated that he would have preferred to have been born female; not that he had any feminine tendencies but he simply hated his penis and would have preferred having a vagina instead. In a prison interview after he was convicted for his heinous crimes, Black confessed to enjoy pushing things up his anus and following his arrest in 1990, police found photographs Black had taken of himself with various unusual objects inserted in his anus. He also confessed to a preoccupation with feces. If one attributed classical Freudian personality psychology, that Black had a tendency to withhold emotion, was oftentimes smelly and messy, and was preoccupied with his anus, then he would be the epitome of an anal personality type.

While in Falkirk, Black was reported as having exposed himself on a number of occasions and, one time, forcibly removing a girl's underwear. At the age of 12 Black made his "first inept attempt at rape." He and two other boys took a girl their age into a field, took off her knickers and lifted her skirt but none were able to "complete the act of penetration." Instead, they touched her vagina and Black admitted that he "forced her to some degree."

After the authorities were called—and had a conference with staff at the Falkirk home—Black was sent to the higher-discipline, all-male Red House in Musselburgh. During his stay there, a male staff member regularly sexually abused him and Black began to solidify his association of sex with dominance and submission.

While in school he developed interests in both swimming and football. Due to poor eyesight he was unable to become a footballer;

however, he was well suited as a lifeguard as he was an excellent swimmer. Further, the sight of young girls in swimsuits fueled his pedophilic fantasies. In fact, 20 years later, when Caroline Hogg was abducted and murdered, her house was en route between the two swimming pools where Black worked as a teenager.

In 1962, when Black was 15, he left the children's home and procured a job as a delivery boy for a butcher. He rented a room in a boys' home in Greenock, near Glasgow, and during this time he admitted to having molested as many as 40 girls while doing his delivery rounds. He claims that when he made a delivery if a young girl was home alone he would sit down and talk to her and then try to touch her.

His first conviction was for lewd and libidinous behavior with a young girl. In 1963, at the age of 17, he approached a seven-year-old girl in a local park and asked her if she would like to accompany him to see some kittens. The naïve girl followed him into a deserted air-raid shelter. He held her by the throat until she lapsed into unconsciousness and he both masturbated over her body and sexually fondled her. She was later found wandering the streets; bleeding, crying, and confused. Black admitted that he didn't know whether she was alive or dead when he left her. Instead of lewd and libidinous behavior, Black should have been charged with and tried for attempted murder. Prior to his 25 June court date, a psychiatric evaluation concluded that this incident was an isolated one and that Black did not need any further treatment.

Black then left Greenock and returned to Grangemouth to start over. After securing employment with a builders' company and renting a room, he finally met his first real girlfriend, Pamela Hodgson. After a physical relationship he fell in love and proposed; however, she broke off the engagement not long after. He was devastated.

In 1966, Black's inappropriate sexual desires resurfaced when he repeatedly molested his landlords' nine-year old granddaughter. While the girl reported it, no charges were filed but Black was asked to leave.

Black returned to his childhood home of Kinlochleven and took a room with a couple who had a seven-year old daughter. Again, he molested the young girl; however, this time the incident was reported and he pled guilty to three counts of indecent assault and was sentenced to a year at Polmont Borstal that was known for rehabilitating the worst of the juvenile criminals. Whereas Black had no problem reiterating all of the aspects of his life and crimes, he has never discussed his time at Borstal, thus leading many to speculate that he was abused during his sentence.

Six months after he was released, Black moved to London and his discovery in child pornography quelled his immediate desire to prey upon young girls. He had discovered that magazines such as *Teenage Sex* and *Lollitots* were clandestinely available, particularly in other countries where pornography laws were less strict such as the Netherlands and he traveled to Amsterdam on several occasions. In fact, when police searched his home after the murders they found over 100 magazines and 50 videotapes depicting child pornography; in addition to Black's own discrete photographs of girls between the ages of eight and 12 he had taken which he kept with his child pornography in a locked suitcase.

Between 1968 and 1970 he held various odd jobs including working as a swimming pool attendant. While here he would oftentimes go underneath the pool, remove the lights, and watch young girls swim. One girl reported that Black had touched her inappropriately and, while no charges were filed, he was fired.

While in London, Black spent considerable time playing darts in pubs—particularly the Three Crowns Pub in Stamford Hill—and became a decent player and a well-known face on the amateur circuit. Many recall Black as a loner who preferred to drink alone irritate others, particularly ladies. During this time Black became acquainted with a Scottish couple named Edward and Kathy Rayson who offered Black lodgings in their empty attic room, which he accepted. He was responsible, albeit reclusive, who—in spite of his poor hygiene—was a model tenant. Although Mrs. Rayson did suspect her lodger of being an avid viewer and reader of pornographic material, neither of the Rayson's thought the material was pedophilic. Black lived with them until his arrest in 1990.

In 1976, after purchasing a white Fiat Transit van, Black secured employment working as a driver for the Hoxton-based Poster Dispatch and Storage, Ltd. that specialized in delivering posters—primarily of music stars—and billboard advertisements. Black would work for PDS for ten years until he was fired due to his constant minor car accidents that cost the company considerable money. Shortly after his dismissal, the company was purchased by two employees who rehired Black because even though he continued to get into accidents, he was a hard worker and was happy to cover for his coworkers by taking the longer runs others didn't care for as they interfered with family commitments. Disturbingly, Black kept a variety of masturbatory tools and girls' clothing which he would don and reenact fantasies in his head; particularly replaying the incident with the seven-year-old girl he had left for dead. When Black committed his first murder it seemed to him like the perfectly natural progression from the fantasy he replayed so frequently.

During his employment, Black became thoroughly familiar with many of London's streets, particularly its minor ones, which would enable him to easily abduct young girls and dump their bodies far from their home without witnesses.

Also during this period, Black changed his appearance multiple time; from shaving his head, growing and/or shaving a beard, and wearing a multitude of different glasses.

The Crimes
Jennifer Cardy, 9
Jennifer Cardy was abducted, sexually assaulted, and murdered on 12 August 1981; a mere two weeks after her ninth birthday. The young

girl was last seen by her mother at 1:40 p.m. when she left her house in the County Antrim village of Ballinderry to ride her bicycle to her friend Louise Major's house. When Cardy didn't return home her family telephoned Major's parents where they were informed that their daughter had never even shown up at their house. Cardy's parents called the police and a search for the missing girl was immediately implemented.

Cardy's bicycle—covered with leaves and branches—was discovered an hour later less than one mile from her home. The kickstand of the bicycle was downwards which suggested that, perhaps, Cardy had stopped to talk to someone—likely her abductor—however, there were no witnesses.

Six days after Cardy's disappearance, two hunters found her body in a dam located close to a dual carriageway in Hillsborough, just 15 miles from her home. Her body displayed evident signs of sexual assault and the autopsy concluded that she had died of drowning that was most likely accompanied by ligature strangulation.

Susan Maxwell, 11

On 20 July 1982, 11-year-old Susan Maxwell from Cornhill on Tweed on the English/Scottish border left her home on her bicycle to play tennis in Coldstream. The two-mile route ensured that Maxwell would know most everyone she passed on the way and it was an area where people looked out for each other, especially the children. A number of local witnesses remembered seeing her until she crossed the bridge spanning the River Tweed.

Maxwell's mother Elizabeth reported her daughter missing after she had driven to the tennis courts to pick her up. One of her daughter's friends said that the two girls parted company outside of the Coldstream police station to walk home their separate ways.

The next day a full-scale search began, involving police and search dogs from both sides of the border. At the height of this search, over 300 officers were assigned full time to locate the young girl with activities including canvasing houses in the area and thorough searching every property within the two towns; over 80 square miles of terrain.

While there were no witnesses to the actual abduction, several people described a white van in the area.

An autopsy concluded that Maxwell had died shortly after her abduction; however, the exact date and time of death remains unknown. Maxwell remained in Black's van, whether alive or dead, for 24 hours as his delivery schedule took him into Edinburgh, Dundee, and Glasgow, where he is known to have made his final scheduled delivery at around midnight. The following day, Black returned from Glasgow to London, and discarded Maxwell's body in a copse near the A518 road near Uttoxeter, Staffordshire; 264 miles from where she was abducted.

On 12 August, Maxwell's body was found by Arthur Meadows, a lorry driver, in a ditch near the A518 road at Loxley, near Uttoxeter, in the Midlands; 250 miles from where Maxwell had been abducted. Her body was fully clothed except for her underwear and shoes and her body had been covered with undergrowth. Due to the advanced state of decomposition, she was identified by dental records. The exact date, time, and cause of death could not be determined. What was known, however, was that Maxwell had been bound, her mouth had been gagged with sticking plaster, and her underwear had been removed and neatly folded beneath her head; thus indicating that she had likely been sexually assaulted before her murder; however, the state of the body precluded knowing for sure what, exactly, happened.

Caroline Hogg, 5

Nearly a year later, five-year-Caroline Hogg became Black's youngest known victim. She disappeared while playing in a park near her Beach Lane home in Portobello—a suburb of Edinburgh—in the early evening of 8 July 1983 after begging her mother Annette for "just five more minutes" of playtime. When Hogg had not come home by

7:15 p.m. her parents and brother looked for her. A young boy around Hogg's age said that he had seen her in the company of a man on the nearby promenade, which her mother and brother frantically searched to no avail. Her mother then called the police and reported her young daughter missing.

An intensive search was undertaken which, at that time, was the largest ever in Scottish history. 2,000 local volunteers and 50 members of the infantry regiment Royal Scots Fusiliers searched all over Portobello and neighboring areas; all the way to Edinburgh. The search also attracted considerable local and national media coverage. In fact, by 10 July, the young girl's disappearance was headline news across the entire United Kingdom. Police interviewed the nine known pedophiles who were in Portobello on the night Hogg disappeared but they were all cleared.

Several eyewitnesses had seen an dirty looking, "bald man who wore glasses" watching Hogg as she played before following her to a nearby fairground named Fun City. 14-year-old Jennifer Booth saw Hogg sitting on a bench with this strange man. Booth heard Hogg reply, "Yes please," to some question posed by the man and assumed that they were father and daughter as they walked toward the fairground while holding hands. At Fun City, the man paid 15 pence for Caroline to ride the children's carousel as he watched her. Afterward, she left the fairground in his company. One child witness stated that she had seemed frightened

Not unlike his other victims, Hogg remained in Black's van for at least 24 hours and her exact date, time, and cause of death remains unknown. Black's schedule showed a poster delivery to Glasgow several hours after Hogg's disappearance and he refueled his vehicle in Carlisle in the wee hours of the following morning.

Hogg's naked body was found on 18 July in a ditch off the A444 road between Northampton to Coventry and close to the M1 motorway in Twycross, Leicestershire; 301 miles from where she had been abducted and a mere 24 miles from where Maxwell's body was discovered the previous year.

Due to advanced decomposition, Hogg was identified by her hair band and locket. The exact cause of death was undetermined; however, the entomologist who examined the body asserted that the body could not have been dumped prior to 12 July, thus suggesting that Black may have disposed of her body while making a delivery to Bedworth on the same date. That she was found completely naked also strongly suggested that her murder was sexual.

The following March, a televised reconstruction of Hogg's abduction was broadcast nationally with the hopes of producing further eyewitnesses. Additionally, all parking tickets issued in Edinburgh were examined, tourists as far as Australia were asked to send in rolls of camera and cine film they had taken in Portobello, police sat for weeks by the A444 taking down registration numbers of all vehicles that passed, and investigators searched the homes of all men identified as having been on the promenade that night for "immoral purposes." After the broadcast, Hogg's parents appealed to the public for any anonymous tips to help them find who killed their daughter. Her father said, "You think it can never happen to you, but it has proven time and time again that it can, and it could again if this man isn't caught in the near future."

Sarah Harper, 10

Three years later, ten-year-old Sarah Harper disappeared from Morley, Leeds, at approximately 7:50 p.m. on 26 March 1986, after she left her home on an errand to purchase a loaf of bread from a local market, the K&M, a mere 100 yards from her home. The shop's owner, Mrs. Champaneri confirmed that the girl did, in fact, purchase a loaf of bread and two packages of crisps at approximately 7:55 p.m. and left at 8:05 p.m. She also stated that a balding man entered her store moments later and left when Harper left.

Harper was last seen by two girls walking into an alley leading towards her Brunswick Place home; a shortcut that locals used. When she had not returned by 8:20 p.m., her mother, Jackie, and sister, Claire, briefly searched the surrounding streets before reporting the young girl missing to West Yorkshire Police at approximately 9:00 p.m. Police—as in the other cases—immediately launched an extensive search for the child with over 100 police officers being assigned full-time to look for the young girl. This search involved house-to-house canvases across Morley; the search of over 3,000 properties; distribution of over 10,000 flyers; and the taking of 1,400 witness statements. Additionally, another 200 local volunteers helped search surrounding areas including the search of a reservoir in nearby Tingley by underwater units.

West Yorkshire Police confirmed that a white Transit van had been seen in the area where Harper had been abducted while two suspicious men had been seen in the vicinity near where Harper walked to the store. One of them was a stocky, balding man. Believing that Harper had likely been abducted the police sent a telex to all forces nationwide requesting that they search the areas where other child murder victims had been found.

At a 3 April press conference, Harper's mother Jackie told journalists that she believed her daughter was dead but that the worst thing was not knowing. Appealing to the abductor, Jackie said, "I just want her back, even if she's dead. If someone would just pick up the phone and tell us where the body is." Afterward, Jackie fainted.

On 19 April, while walking his dog, a man named David Moult found Sarah's naked body, gagged and bound, floating in the River Trent near Nottingham, nearly seventy miles from where she was kidnapped.

An autopsy revealed that while the cause of death was drowning, she sustained injuries to her head and neck which likely rendered her unconscious before she was thrown into the water. In addition to being beaten, the evidence demonstrated that Harper had been the victim of a violent and sustained sexual assault—including being sodomized—prior to being tossed into the river. The pathologist described these pre-mortem injuries as "simply terrible." The young victim's father, Terry, Jackie's ex-husband, had to identify his daughter's body and stated that "it was worse than I ever dreamed of."

Investigation and Arrest

By the spring of 1983, whereas many detectives assigned to the inquiry into Maxwell's murder were assigned elsewhere, several detectives did, in fact, remain on the case. When Hogg's body was found in July 1983, Detective Chief Superintendent of Staffordshire Police Dennis Boden held an emergency meeting with senior Staffordshire and Leicestershire detectives to explore the possibility that the same person was responsible for both murders.

Cardy's murder would not be formally linked to the other cases until 2009.

Due to the distance between where the victims were abducted and subsequently found, police suspected that the same person was responsible and that he worked in an occupation that required extensive travel across the United Kingdom, such as a lorry or van driver, or some type of sales representative. Additionally, that both victims were bound and likely subjected to sexual assault—and were clad in white ankle socks when they disappeared—it was presumed that this triggered some sort of fetish response by the perpetrator. It was also decided that due to the circumstantial and geographical nature of the crimes that the perpetrator was likely an opportunist.

Further, since both Maxwell and Hogg were abducted on a Friday, the perpetrator most likely had some sort of delivery or production schedule. After discovery of the bodies, police contacted all transport firms with deliveries in Scotland and the Midlands and all drivers were questioned as to their whereabouts on the dates of the abductions; however, this tactic failed to uncover any potential leads.

Complete cooperation existed between police from the four separate police departments involved in the manhunt. Initially, a satellite incident room that was based in Coldstream coordinated the collective efforts for leads in the Maxwell case while additional incident rooms in Leith and Portobello coordinate the search for evidence in Hogg's case. However, within hours of the discovery of Hogg's body, there was overwhelming consensus that both cases were linked and that they should join efforts with one investigating officer to coordinate all inquiries. Assistant Chief Constable of Northumbia Police Hector Clark was appointed to lead the investigation. Clark established incident rooms in Northumberland and Leith police stations to coordinate all efforts to search for the girls' murderer.

Initially, all information related to both cases was logged with a card-filing system that initially grew to over 500,000 index cards just for the Maxwell case alone. Being familiar with the criticism levied against police during the Yorkshire Ripper case for their being overwhelmed due to the sheer volume of information filed with this type of system, Clark introduced computerized technology into the investigation. Collective use of a computerized database that everyone involved in the investigation could access would improve results. Thus, by December 1986, all of the information related to the three murders (thus far) would be entered into the HOLMES information technology system and additional information would continue to be entered so that police forces nationwide would be able to cross-check all data entered into the system. Initially, detectives looked at individuals who had been convicted of serious sexual crimes against children within the ten years prior to Maxwell's murder in 1982 be further investigated. The list of potential suspects was narrowed to 40,000; however, Black's name never arose as his only conviction was in 1967.

Eventually, this database that was based at the Child Murder Bureau in the West Yorkshire city of Bradford would expand to hold information on over 187,000 individuals; 220,000 vehicles; and 57,000 witness interviews. Much of the information in the database had been obtained through three confidential hotlines established in 1984 by the inquiry team which eventually enabled police to solve numerous other, unrelated crimes, including child abuse offenses.

Several days after Harper's abduction and murder, a witness contacted West Yorkshire Police to inform authorities that on 26 March, at approximately 9:15 p.m., he had seen a white van parked close to the River Soar. A stocky, balding man was standing by the passenger door. Because the River Soar is a tributary to the River Trent and that the vehicle's and man's descriptions were similar to those given by other witnesses, investigators took this account seriously. Furthermore, Black is known to have refueled his van in the Newport Pagnell, Buckinghamshire, the following afternoon; which may suggest that he had taken Harper to the village of Ratcliffe on Soar and had discarded her body in the river either in the evening of the day she was abducted or in the early hours the following morning. Because Harper's abductor likely traveled on the M1 motorway before disposing of her body, investigators from both West Yorkshire and Nottinghamshire Police Departments questioned motorists and staff at all service stations along the M1 motorway between Woolley and Trowell as to whether they might have seen anything unusual on the 26th or 27th of March. Staff at one service station did, in fact, remember a white Transit van that had "seemed out of place" on the evening of 26 March; however, they could not provide a clear description of the driver.

Clark initially did not believe that Harper's murder was connected to Maxwell's and Hogg's due to several dissimilarities; however, in retrospect there were glaring and perhaps more telling similarities. All of the victims were young girls skillfully abducted from public places for sexual purposes and they were driven south and murdered. Further, the three bodies were found within 26 miles of each other in a triangular area known as the Midlands Triangle. Even though Harper's sexual assault appeared to be more vicious than the other two, experts assert that serial killers frequently increase their violence as the murderer gains more confidence and requires more brutality to achieve and maintain arousal. Eight months after Harper was found, Her Majesty's Inspector of Constabulary determined that all three murders were, in fact, linked and that one database be established. Entering all information into a single database took three years and was completed in July 1990.

In 1986, investigators formally requested assistance from the FBI to create a profile of their perpetrator which was completed in January 1988. This profile described the killer as a 30- to 40-year-old white male, likely a loner, who would likely be unkempt in appearance and had received less than 12 years of formal education. He probably lived alone, rented his home, and was in a middle-class neighborhood. Additionally, the profile surmised that the murderer's motives were purely sexual and that he likely had a fixation or obsession with child pornography. Profilers also hypothesized that the killer retained souvenirs from his victims and likely engaged in necrophilia with his victims' bodies shortly after their deaths.

Black was arrested on 14 July 1990, near Stow, Scotland, after snatching six-year-old Mandy Wilson off of the street and bundling her into his van. An alert neighbor, 53-year-old retired postmaster David Herkes, took down the van's registration number and called the police. After a chase, Black was apprehended. The victim was actually the daughter of one of the police officers on the scene and he discovered his daughter in the back of the van, bound and gagged, and stuffed into a sleeping bag. Prior to tying her up, Black had sexually assaulted her. Black was charged with plagium (kidnapping).

When Black's residence was searched, investigators discovered a large collection of child pornography.

Trial and Sentencing

In August 1990, Black was tried and convicted of kidnapping Wilson and given a life sentence. The sentence was based, largely, upon psychiatrists' testimony that Black would continue to pose a great threat to young girls.

Black was still the prime suspect in the murders of Susan Maxwell, Caroline Hogg, and Sarah Harper. Clark decided to interview Black as he was already serving a life sentence for the Wilson kidnapping and Clark mentioned that when he first saw him his gut feeling was that Black was his man. However, instinct and a gut feeling are not good enough for procuring a guilty conviction in a court of law. Black spoke candidly about his prior convictions, about his short relationship with his fiancée, about the sexual abuse he had endured as a child, about his fantasy life, and about his masturbatory practices. When asked specific questions about the three murders he fell silent.

A check of Black's gas receipts and delivery schedules placed him in the vicinity of each girl's abduction and he was charged with all three murders, as well as the attempted kidnapping of a 15-year-old girl who had escaped from the man who tried to drag her into his van in 1988. In this case, on 28 April 1988, 15-year-old Teresa Thornhill had been walking home from the park where she had met friends when Thornhill noticed a blue van stopped ahead. When the driver asked her for help and she denied, he had grabbed her from behind and was taking her to his van. She recalled that he was sweaty and stinky and was able to grab his testicles while screaming. Her friend Andrew, hearing her screams, came to help his friend and chase the assailant away.

Black's murder trial began on 13 April 1994 in front of Judge William MacPherson. Black pled not guilty to the ten charges levied against him which included murder, kidnapping, and preventing the lawful burial of a body. Despite his denial of any guilt, the prosecution was able to place him at each scene and to demonstrate similarities between the three murders and the prior kidnapping for which he had already been convicted and sentenced. His trial lasted five weeks.

On 19 May, the jury found Black guilty of all charges and he was sentenced to life imprisonment with a minimum of 35 years for each charge, to be served concurrently; thus rendering him 82 years old before being eligible for parole—if he were still alive at that time.

On 15 December, Black had been served a formal summons charging him with the murder and sexual assault of Jennifer Cardy and his second murder trial began at Armagh Crown Court on 22 September 2011 before Judge Ronald Weatherup. As he did regarding his other three victims, Black pled not guilty.

Evidence such as gas receipts and delivery schedules demonstrated that Black was in the area at the time Cardy disappeared. This second trial lasted six weeks and on 27 October 2011 he was found guilty of abducting, murdering, and sexually assaulting Cardy. He was given another life sentence.

Aftermath

Black suffered a fatal heart attack while incarcerated at HMP Maghaberry on 12 January 2016, just weeks before he was to be charged with the murder of 13-year-old Genette Tate who had disappeared while delivering newspapers on 19 August 1978 in Aylesbeare, Devon, England.

Senior detectives believe that Black was responsible for eight deaths, in addition to the Tate case; however, 12 other child murders committed across the UK, Ireland, and continental Europe between 1969 and 1987 have also been linked to Black. These include: April Fabb, 13, 8 April 1969, UK; Christine Markham, 9, 21 May 1973, UK; Suzanne Lawrence, 14, 22 July 1979, UK; Patricia Morris, 14, 16 June 1980, UK; Pamela Hastie, 16, 4 November 1981, UK; Mary Boyle, 6, 18 March 1977, Ireland; Silke Garben, 10, 20 June 1985, Germany; Cheryl Morriën, 7, 5 August 1986, Netherlands; Virginie Delmas, 10, 5 May 1987, France; Hemma Devy-Greedharry, 10, 30 May 1987, France; Perrine Vigneron, 7, 3 June 1987, France; and Sabine Dumont, 9, 27 June 1987, France. In all of these cases, Black is known to have been in the area or a white van with a driver who resembled Black was seen.

Prior to his death, Black never admitted culpability in any of the murders for which he was convicted and suspected.

His body was cremated on 29 January and his ashes were discarded at sea.